# THE EXQUISITE RISK

"Perfect for reading at the beach—or anytime you feel the urge to be surprised by the lyrical suddenness of life."
            —*Yoga Journal*

"Meant to be savored like a fine meal. Nepo's book is filled with poetic imagery and language, enticing the reader to linger over its delicate flavors. Filtered through his personal experience, Nepo pours wisdom from the chalice of many cultures and faiths."
            —*Cleveland Plain Dealer*

"In this exquisite book, the suffering of one man speaks with the voice of wisdom and beauty to all of us."
            —Jacob Needleman, author of *The American Soul, A Little Book on Love,* and *Money and the Meaning of Life*

"Every page of *The Exquisite Risk* is alive with Mark's compassion, rich with his soulfulness. If you are looking for one of those rare books that offer companionship on the journey, you will find none better than this."
            —Parker J. Palmer, bestselling author of *A Hidden Wholeness, The Courage to Teach,* and *Let Your Life Speak*

"An inspiration . . . *The Exquisite Risk* affirms that there are essentially two responses to life—a risky opening up to love and a controlling move into success and isolation. The direct reporting of Mark Nepo's epiphanies moves and flows in a wonderful sequencing of revelations that deepen and fill out as we read. . . . An exquisite gift."
            —Robert Inchausti, author of *The Ignorant Perfection of Ordinary People*

# THE
# EXQUISITE
# RISK

Daring to Live an

Authentic Life

# MARK NEPO

THREE RIVERS PRESS · NEW YORK

THREE RIVERS PRESS and the tugboat design are registered trademarks of
Random House, Inc.

Originally published in harcover in the United States by Harmony Books, an imprint of
the Crown Publishing Group, a division of Random House, Inc., New York, in 2005.

Portions of this work have previously appeared in slightly different
form in *Pilgrimage: Reflections on the Human Journey*
and *Sufi: A Journal of Sufism.*

Library of Congress Cataloging-in-Publication Data
Nepo, Mark.
The exquisite risk : daring to live an authentic life / Mark Nepo.
Includes bibliographical references.
1. Self-actualization (Psychology). I. Title.
BF637.S4N46 2005
158.1—dc22
2004018138

ISBN 0-307-33584-4

Printed in the United States of America

*Design by JoAnne Metsch*

10   9   8   7

First Paperback Edition

# TO MY READER

For years , I've been trying to explore and understand: How can we, being forgetfully human, remember we are of one human family? How can we stay awake and authentic when our wounds make us numb and hidden? How can we minimize what stands between us and our experience of life? How can we make a practice of wearing down what thickens around our mind and heart? How can this practice of staying authentic serve and draw strength from the universal Whole while we are immersed and entangled in the moment of our lives?

As a cancer survivor, I have found myself like Lazarus, awake again, in the same earthly place but different. Everything has changed and nothing has changed. This wakefulness has led me to be a student of that vibrant edge where our inner life meets the world. Being a poet and philosopher, I find myself there with a particular set of tools to search with.

But we all live on this shore between the depths of being and the dangers of experience. This book has become a journal of the challenges and gifts of being a spirit in the world. It has taken three years to birth this book, and I view it as an intimate companion in exploring the intoxicating quandaries of being alive. When struggling through my illness, I was bereft at how many of the books I owned were useless. Ever since, I have been committed to finding and creating books that can help us live. It is my devout hope that this book is such a help.

# CONTENTS

We cannot change the world by a new plan, project, or idea. We cannot even change other people by our convictions, stories, advice and proposals, but we can offer a space where people are encouraged to disarm themselves, lay aside their occupations and preoccupations and listen with attention and care to the voices speaking in their own center.

—HENRI NOUWEN

Work of seeing is done.
Now practice heart-work . . .

—RILKE

# OPENING THE GIFT

Before stories were recorded, what happened to the living was told and retold around fires, on cliffs, and in the shade of enormous trees. And it is said that somewhere on the edge of what was known and unknown, a man and a woman paused in their struggles to survive and faced each other. One asked the other, "Is there more to this than hauling wood?" The older of the two sighed, "Yes . . . and no."

This may have been the beginning of our sense of being and our search for meaning. I imagine these two faced everything we face. For the journey is the same: how to open our pain and listen to all that matters, so we can make it through and rejoice from day to day.

Like those before us, we have the chance to wake and love, the chance to welcome the gift of surprise and befriend the Whole. For beneath the life of problem-solving waits the struggle to be real, from which no one is exempt. We each are asked to make our way through the drama of our bleeding to the stripping of our will, through the tensions of our suffering to the humility of surrender where we might learn the ordinary art of living at the pace of what is real.

So, is there more to this than hauling the wood of our history around? More than just replaying our patterns? Whether yesterday or five thousand years ago, there has always been the need to break our habits in the world—the need to give up what no longer works.

Ultimately, there is always the need to risk being new. Yet even succeeding, to be authentic—living as close to our experience as possible—is arduous. For being human, we remember and forget. We stray and return, fall down and get up, and cling and let go, again and again. But it is this straying and returning that makes life interesting, this clinging and letting go—damned as it is—that exercises the heart.

They say that, after a time, the two who paused on the edge of what was known and unknown stumbled into humility. "Please, tell me, is there more to this than hauling wood?" the one would ask again. And the more tired of the two replied, "No, no. It is *all* in the hauling, *all* in the wood, *all* in how we face each other around the small fires we can build."

It was then that they rested, as we rest, when accepting the grace of our humanness. You see, we've always been on a journey, like it or not, aware of it or not, struggling to enter and embrace things as they are. And when we can accept our small part in the way of things, when we can build a small fire and gather, it opens us to joy. So join me on this journey we are already on. We can help each other hold nothing back. We can help each other live a sincere life. We can help each other wear down what gets in the way, waking close to the bone.

Come. There are teachers everywhere: in the stories around us, in the stories within us, in the life of expression that sings where we are broken, in the kinship of gratitude that keeps reminding us that we need each other as we become the earth.

# MOVEMENT 1

*There Are*
*Teachers*
*Everywhere*

# LISTENING TO THE
# VOICE INSIDE

*If I dare to hear you,*
*I will feel you like the sun*
*and grow in your direction.*

I remember the first time I was forced to listen, not by adults or teachers, but by running as a boy in the playground so fast and free that I fell and scraped my knee. After the cut reduced to a throb, I couldn't get up. It was then that I saw my blood sprinkled in the dirt. It was then I first realized that this great thing we ran on was the earth. I had never paid attention to it. I was just a boy. I put my ear to the ground and listened. I don't know what I thought I would hear. But it was summer and the ground was warm. So I thought I heard warmth. I told my teacher, but she said you can't hear warmth. Yet some forty-five years later, I think you can. Whenever you put your ear to the earth or to your own heart, the deeper instruments play, swelling our sense of things. When lost, we simply have to remember to put our ear to the earth, or to our heart, and we will hear a warmth that guides.

The next time, I was more drawn to listen than forced. It was a few years later on my father's sailboat, which was the oasis of my youth. It was a thirty-foot ketch that he'd built. Once out to sea, I remember being pulled forward by the water till the family noises faded. I found myself sitting in the bow of the boat, legs over the side, staring into the endless waves parting around us. I didn't have the words or concepts for it, but it felt like God's voice murmuring in the waves. This was my first experience of solitude.

At a very early age, both the earth and the sea opened me to something deep inside that has carried me ever since. It was years before I had names for any of this, and after years of study in many spiritual traditions, I believe it is the simple, mysterious pulse of what is sacred.

In these small childhood experiences of listening, I discovered a spiritual law: that we are both forced and drawn by everything larger than us to hear what is essential. Repeatedly, we are given chance after chance to stop and listen to all that is fundamental. When forced to our knees, we are offered the chance to hear the warmth in all that holds us up. When drawn into the rhythms of vastness that surround us, we are offered the chance to hear the waves of God's voice, of which we are one, if we can leave the noise of others behind.

When we can listen deeply, we are strengthened to feel that everything around us lives within us *and* that everything within us lives as part of the world. When we experience both the circum- ference and center of the circle of life at once, we are then in the larger Self, the Universal Self, as Carl Jung describes it.

Imagine a nineteen-year-old in the chaos of war, running through mud and explosions, seeing others fall around him. Imag- ine him slipping into a ditch, a small pocket of stillness that seems out of reach, for the moment, from all the destruction. And in that small empty space between the mud and his frightened mouth, he is forced to listen to his breath. In that small cloud emitting from his lungs, he is forced to hear the breath of everything that ever lived. The conflicts change and the ditches change, but sometimes listening to that small breath is all we have. And sometimes it opens up everything.

This falling down and emptying ourselves of noise so that we can hear the sacred pulse of things is at the heart of all the meditation practices invoked throughout the ages. Sooner or later, if we want to *feel* what it is to be alive in a Universe that is alive, we will have to empty ourselves, open our hearts, and listen. This emptying and opening and listening is the practice that allows us to hear that voice of God (whatever name you give to it) that resides in each of us. By listening with all of who we are, we are briefly illuminated, like stained glass, letting everything move through us in those privileged and enlightened moments.

But how do we listen? It is so simple and so hard. So obvious to begin and so elusive to maintain. In this lies the vitality of deep listening. *To keep beginning.* Over and over. *To keep emptying and opening.* And simply *to keep listening.* For to listen is to continually give up all expectation and to give our attention, completely and freshly, to what is before us, not really knowing what we will hear or what that will mean. In the practice of our days, to listen is to lean in, softly, with a willingness to be changed by what we hear.

Over the years, I have been opened to a deeper listening when called to sit with the dying. In the sacred air between us, I have heard the weight of things fall away, have seen ancient hands that held me as a boy search for something that has always been near, have wondered what hundred-year-old eyes see with their last look.

I remember my grandmother at ninety-four staring into some holy place I couldn't see. It was the moment after I'd left. I had turned back for one more taste of her. She didn't know I was there, and I saw her as devoutly amazed as any reluctant prophet. Somewhere between the bedpan and her dirty window, eternity was singing. I'll never forget her face.

It seems that those pared down to only what is essential peer into the one untranslatable place, the sweet place that no one can speak of. And when waking on the edge of life or death, when pressed to be fully here, we peer into a truth that changes every-thing. Then, if still here, we come back with our hearts seared anew by that seeing. If blessed, we come back to live in days that say so sweetly that everything, even dust, is beautifully ordinary and irreplaceable.

We can't seek out such wakefulness. In truth, it happens to us. But we can ready ourselves for such privileged moments. We can, if present enough, listen to each day the way we would listen to those who are dying. We can keep beginning, keep emptying, keep breathing ourselves open.

# THE PRACTICE OF
# BEING HUMAN

*As a man in his last breath*
*drops all he is carrying*

*each breath is a little death*
*that can set us free.*

It's Friday afternoon and the sun is out, but I have so much on my desk and if I stay till six or seven, I can start next week ahead of things. But the sun is so bright and my heart is begging me to burst into the day. And now a small yellowish bird, so bright, is flirting at my window.

Each of us in our own way faces these choices daily: To save or spend? To earn or experience? To get ahead or leave nothing behind? To attend the tasks that others set out for us or to attend the undiscovered edge of what it means to be alive? Of course, we e·· must *survive*, must pay the rent or mortgage and feed oursel· pay for the heat. And we each must *thrive*, must pay atte·· where the shifting river of life turns, so we do not lose our ·

So, this is not about bemoaning or rebelling against th·· ties that keep our feet to the ground. Rather, I want to open· versation about the pain and joy of being awake. I want to inq·· into the personal practice of being authentic, of being fully here, of being human. I want to know how we as spirits, as walking pieces of divinity, can suffer our limitations with dignity and rejoice in the often gritty mystery of our humanness.

We often feel compelled to sacrifice or postpone the seeds of joy in favor of a practicality that we hope will insure a secure future. I myself was a great saver. I had a firm will that could defer the sudden urge for new music into a fund for the unexpected emergency lurking out of view. But then the unexpected came and I was ill. Now, on the other side, my mind has been reformed and deferring anything that might ignite joy, that might help loved ones grow *now*, deferring *anything real*, seems dangerous.

Oh, I still make sure there's enough for the mortgage and I've never been one to buy a lot of things, but surviving has reframed the entire notion of wealth for me. Once waking into the realization that eternity is waiting in every moment, I discovered that wealth is *time*, not money. And money becomes a tool, a sort of changing shovel that digs into the moment at hand until the ever-present roots of life are found and fed.

So, again, questions arise: Are we here to achieve or to experience? To be good or authentic? To build for tomorrow or dig into today? To save for a perfect future or to fuel a flawed but loving present? *Just what is the nature of our work once awake?*

I recently returned from facilitating a retreat for corporate bankers. I confess I had my stereotypes and hesitations, but after a short time discovered that they were good, caring people who excel at what they do. They, too, were searching for a way to unwall and unwind into the quiet essence that seems to be so far away from the hive of their excellence. The more we talked, the more we could see that their jobs require them to be skillful at *risk management*, while their lives require them to be masterful at *risk enhancement*. I realized by the end of the day that their tension in doing what they do and being who they are is really the same for us all. It is not either-or. We each face the challenge to both survive *and* thrive, to be cautious and daring at once.

It seems that, whether we are bankers or florists or mechanics, the work of wakefulness is not to drop what we do, but to inhabit it more completely, holding nothing back. Our task, then, is to live out the paradox of being opened and closed and to hold open the mysterious space in between.

I know firsthand that the precautions of a lifetime can be punctured in an instant. I remember preparing for my second chemo treatment and being given Atavan, a drug that would give me short-term amnesia. Since my first chemo treatment was very painful and exhausting, I was afraid to re-enter the strange darkness that everyone was saying would make me well. At the time, the terms of life were shifting. The future was eroding and I was being forced to reassess in what dimension I was truly living.

The treatment was thankfully uneventful, and in its aftermath I was left alone while my loved ones shared their relief. But within weeks, all sorts of tickets arrived in the mail: to concerts, Broadway shows, and most curious—six round-trip tickets to St. Martin in the Caribbean. While left alone, I had called and charged all these things to our credit card! I still have no memory of this!

But the lasting lesson is that, reduced to *Now*, some deeper part of me began to live, holding nothing back. It is a moment that changed my life. And through that deeper part, I began to see that we are delivered through all these gifts and tensions until we are honed by experience into something more and more vulnerable and beautiful.

I returned everything but the tickets to St. Martin. I placed them near the candle by my bed and vowed that, if I lived through this, my loved ones and I would go. And we did.

So, here I am. It's Friday afternoon and the sun is out, but I have so much on my mind and if I stay, I can start next week ahead of things. But the sun is so bright and my heart is begging me to burst into the day. And all my loved ones are calling. And I wonder why it is so hard to put things down and live.

# THE NATURE
# OF THE DANCE

*Death pushed me to the edge.*
*Nowhere to back off. And*
*to the shame of my fears,*
*I danced with abandon*
*in his face. I never*
*danced as free.*

*And Death backed off,*
*the way dark backs off*
*a sudden burst of flame.*
*Now there's nothing left*
*but to keep dancing.*

*It is the way*
*I would have chosen*
*had I been born*
*three times*
*as brave.*

That dance is what we're here to explore. That dance is the
vibrant, life-giving act of spirit and how it expresses us. Whether it
appears as a cry of pain or a song of joy, this unseeable presence is
the lifeblood of our health. As blood must circulate through a
body for that body to be vital, as water must pass through the gills

for a fish to stay alive, the dance of spirit must move through us if we are to know and feel our place in the mysterious scheme of things. For it is the dance of spirit that opens us to who we are. In this way, the act of being who we are is at the heart of staying well.

So, let's talk about the nature of the dance. To begin with, why is being who we are essential to staying well? Because we must meet the outer world with our inner world or existence will crush us. It is a spiritual law, as real as gravity. If we don't assume our space as living beings, the rest of life will fill us completely the way water fills a hole.

Then, how do we assume our presence and inhabit our living space? It seems that this requires another, more personal form of meeting in which our inner life helps to define our outer life; where who we are shapes what we do.

This meeting of our inner and outer lives is called integrity, and the health of our integrity often determines our inner strength and resilience in meeting the outer world. This is the purpose of integrity: to balance the outer forces of existence with the inner forces of spirit.

One of the most useful definitions of integrity comes from Rabbi Jonathan Omer-Man:

Integrity is the ability to listen to a place inside oneself that doesn't change, even though the life that carries it may change.

Still, what do we mean by a place inside that doesn't change? For we are not defining integrity as a license to stubbornly adhere to our own point of view. Rather, we are offering a sense that goes deeper than what we've been taught or even what we've experienced. This deeper place inside that doesn't change serves as a threshold to an Original Presence we all share. It is an inlet to Wholeness and all that is larger than us. Given the chance, that place inside will speak to each of us. In essence, the soul's calling is to keep dancing and listening to that Original Presence that doesn't change.

Of course, being human, things get in the way. We often get in our own way, repeatedly. In truth, we all struggle with these recurring life positions:

*To journey without being changed is to be a nomad.*
*To change without journeying is to be a chameleon.*
*To journey and be transformed by the journey is to be a pilgrim.*

It would be easy to see the first two positions as bad or at least counterproductive. But all three are unavoidable. We cycle through them as part of the human process, as part of our unending path to and from integrity—both in our personal landscape and in finding our balanced place in the Universe. It is our continual efforts to live from the pilgrim position that keep us close to the pulse of what is sacred.

In truth, listening deeply and inwardly allows us to keep meeting the outer world with our inner being, and this mysteriously keeps us and the world vital. Often, the nature of the dance cycles us from being self-centered to being other-centered to being balanced as an integral part in an integrated whole. And when we're blessed to experience those balanced, integrated moments, it becomes clear that everything is relational. Everything inside us and between us is circulatory—an ongoing exchange of what matters.

My own transformation as a poet speaks to this. As a young man, I started with the ambition to be a great artist. The everlasting poem was the goal. When I had cancer, though, my writing became a rope of self-expression by which I climbed into tomorrow. For instance, the poem that began this chapter came to me while being wheeled into surgery. I kept staring at the fluorescent ceilings whipping by, the IV draping off my arm, while some voice larger than my frightened self kept saying, *There's nothing left but to keep dancing.*

And so, greatness became irrelevant. Waking was a triumph. Now my ambition, if you can still call it that, is the great chance to be. It's all given way to a different experience of expression—one that goes beyond the writing of poems or the creating of art. I now see that expression—with ourselves, each other, and God—is a constant way of tuning our instrument of being, of staying faithful to that place inside that doesn't change. But expression is more than just the mouthing of words. It is the exchange of what matters between living things.

In this regard, expression can be the placing of bread on the pathway of birds. It is simply the way we exchange vitality—the way that plants and humans exchange oxygen and carbon dioxide, each giving the other what it needs to live. In a daily way, the exchange of what matters is the dance by which we stay alive and true.

# THE EXQUISITE RISK

The exquisite risk to still our own house . . .

—St. John of the Cross

At any moment, if quiet enough and open enough, we can drop into the fabric of existence in which everything, even pain, has its vivid signature of energy that we call, at different times, truth or beauty or peace.

It is from this ground of being that we know and feel the unseeable web of connection between all life. It is from here that we see more clearly, below the tensions of our wants and disappointments.

The exquisite risk that St. John speaks of is twofold: the risk to still our own house so that Spirit can come through, so that we might drop into the vital nature of things, and the risk to then let that beautiful knowing inform our days.

The risk is exquisite because it holds open the veil before which is hell-on-earth and behind which is heaven-on-earth. For without knowing and feeling our connection to all life, the patterns of experience seem to make no sense. From within that knowing connection, though, we can feel the tug and pull of everything alive. This does not eliminate pain, but distributes its acuteness, the way a net softens the impact of a fall. Without this feeling of connection, we bump through life blindly, startled by the suddenness of things. With it, we can place ourselves in a landscape teeming with meaning, just waiting to be lived into.

The exquisite risk is a doorway, then, that lets us experience the extraordinary in the ordinary. It is always near. Truth opens it. Love opens it. Humility opens it. And if stubborn, pain will intensify to open it. Sadness can open it, if felt to its center. Silence and time open it, if we enter them and don't just watch them.

In the same way that watching the surface of water can be mesmerizing and yet it does not reveal what waits below, the busyness and drama of the world can keep us from going below the surface of the very moments that are ours to enter. In my life, I have known truth and beauty and peace to be ever-present companions that I often sit beside, bemoaning their absence.

So often, the risk that leads to revelation and then courage is, at first, a very quiet threshold that we must dare to cross, through which life waits like a secret hidden in the open. This quiet risk somehow reminds us that there is *nothing between us*, nothing between the oceans and our hearts, between the sands and our eyes, between the infinite sufferings and splendors that make up the breathing world of life on earth. Though often unseen and often unheard, everything living affects everything else. The net is incredibly wide. We are not alone—for all its comforts and fears— we are not alone.

Once risking our way through that threshold, we inevitably fall back into the streets. But we are blessed with a consciousness that knows that life consists of this shimmer between depth and surface, between oneness and isolation. Here, the exquisite risk becomes the courage of heart not to forget, not to believe that the extraordinary center of things has vanished because we have lost touch with it.

You see, the exquisite risk is really a sensibility more than a circumstance, more a way of entering and carrying Spirit through our days than a skillful response to a fleeting opening.

Often, we know it is near when the eyes of a stranger or a distant loved one cause us to linger, when the ache we've suppressed for weeks creeps into our throat, when silence appears at the edge of our exhaustion like an old friend we couldn't find. Often, the exquisite risk is waiting on the other side of the curtains we draw and the invitations we decline. And sudden birds, if followed, will lead us there. If we only enter our picture of life and let go of the frame.

# THE STRANGE
# STORYTELLER

*Say it. Say it.*
*The Universe is made of stories,*
*not atoms.*

—MURIEL RUKEYSER

For years, behind the first house I lived in on my own, there was an old oak which had a piece of barbed wire embedded in the center of its trunk. The tree had grown around the wire until it seemed as if the wire were some hard artery in the heart of the tree. I often wonder, how did this happen? Obviously, the wire must have been loose at one time. Just when did the tree start to grow around it? At what point did the tree incorporate the wire into its woody grain? It strikes me now that this holds a truth about our need to tell our story, about our need to voice what happens to us. For the longer we keep secrets and don't tell our story, the more we grow ourselves around the pain of what is not told, and the harder it is to pull the wire from our heart. It can be done, but it is always more painful once the heart has knit the wire of our secrets into its tissue.

The truth is that telling heals. Not just once, but as a way of being that filters the heart of its debris. In the way that ecosystems flush out the buildup of compost, storytelling is a God-given way to make an ecosystem of the heart, to flush out the buildup of scar tissue and compost that clogs our being. This is one fundamental purpose of human voice: to irrigate the heart dammed up with experience.

And once the telling begins, experience becomes a strange storyteller. Often, it shows us how to lose and how to heal. Often, it shows us how to face what seems unfaceable. Events stranger than dream come into being and we are left to find the medicine in them, which is only released by the telling. Just what stories unfolding today will be the myths by which we learn tomorrow? Whole lives can be turned by the story of one time unlocking the truth of another.

For instance, once a stretch of wire has grown in the heart, what will it take to finally disintegrate it? This reminds me of another tree story that I heard in Pennsylvania. After a day of getting to know each other, a sixty-year-old surgeon told me how his great-great-grandmother's uncle stopped haying in the middle of the day, hooked his scythe in the crook of a tree, and walked off to fight at Gettysburg, never to return. He told me how no one ever took the scythe down. How the handle of that scythe fell apart, but the heart of that tree grew around the blade. Just as my tree grew around the wire. Just as the heart of our nation grew around that devastating battle. He told me how, for a hundred years, a stubborn vengeance fueled his family and, for just as long, the tree stubbornly looked like it was growing a blade. He softened to tell me how, after his parents died, he felt compelled to bring black and white children to see the blade and touch the tree. He was almost in tears as he told me how, after they did, the blade one day crumbled and the tree grew a new limb.

And a Basque woman told me how it's in her heritage to endure until you see. When I asked for more, she told me of her great-grandfather whose whaling ship went to pieces off the coast of South Africa. How he eventually sent word to his wife, who walked for two years carrying enough money to build another ship. How she walked down the Pyrenees. How she boated past Gibraltar. How she followed the Nile. By the time she walked the continent, she'd seen so many fighting over things that didn't matter, that when she appeared one day in the South African sun, she dropped the money in his lap and simply said, "Please, stop all this and just come home."

And where is home? Is it where we begin or where we end up? Is it where we long to be or where life puts us to make good use of our gifts? Recently, an Asian man living in Minnesota told me of his grandfather who, on his way home to China during World War II, couldn't get through and wound up living in Hong Kong. How, when free schools were banned there, he realized why he was led to Hong Kong and opened a rooftop school where children could learn while staring at the sky. From that point on, Hong Kong was his home. Then he told me that when he goes home, he visits a school there named after his grandfather.

In my own life, it was just a small moment, years ago, in which I understood where I come from. I sat in the yard where I grew up, where the bully had hammered me, where school had come and gone, and the mimosa, which was there when I was born, died. It seemed that very day, but that was only when we noticed. My father had a small pit beneath the tree and every summer he'd set fires at night and the cinders would drift up and burn the leaves. The tree seemed to grow out of reach, as best it could. But my father wouldn't move the pit. And now it had died. We stared up at it. My father said it was the years of flame that choked it, then set another fire beneath it. It grew late, and he slept, an aging man with a stubborn wound I never quite understood. He looked tenacious, on fire himself, even when asleep. My mother caught me watching him and she shook her head at the stubborn will that coats our house. How we sit in things we build and ruin.

In truth, we often make small choices that matter greatly, and we can use all the guidance we can get. From others, yes, but also from life itself. As sailors have read the currents of the sea for centuries, experience, if seen as such an ocean, can reveal the currents we find ourselves in. And how we read the geography of stories that surrounds us—the stories of people, moments, and places—this is our compass.

Whether through the patterns left in snow, or geese honking in the dark, or through the brilliant wet leaf that hits your face the moment you are questioning your worth, the quiet teachers are everywhere, pointing us to the unlived portion of our lives. When we think we are in charge, the lessons dissolve as accidents or coincidence. But when we're humble enough to welcome the connections, the glass that breaks across the room is offering us direction, giving us a clue to the story we are in.

# YOU MUST REVERSE
# THE HAIKU

*The bottom of the sky*
*sings the ancient ways*
*till I give the truth away . . .*

In the 1600s, the Japanese master Basho spoke profoundly to his student Kikakou:

> We shouldn't abuse God's creatures.
> You must reverse your haiku, not:

> > a dragonfly;
> > remove its wings—
> > pepper tree.
> > but:

> > a pepper tree;
> > add wings to it—
> > dragonfly.

The destruction or healing of the world hinges on how this thought unfolds. Whether we pull things apart or put things together makes all the difference. Indeed, Basho's small instruction reveals how human history has unfolded, with one pilgrim taking things apart and another putting them back together, and on and on. As Martin Luther King Jr. prophesied, "I believe what the self-centered have torn down, the other-centered will build up."

Yet we must be watchful, for we all suffer both the impulse to separate and own and the impulse to unify and belong. Just as our eyes shut and open repeatedly, we take things apart and put them together constantly. Still, healing often depends on keeping things joined the way that wakefulness depends on keeping our eyes open.

So much of our life on earth depends on how we relate to everything around us. And while there are certainly times when it is necessary to dismantle bonds or entanglements to regain the health of freedom, mostly, when we can put things together instead of taking things apart, we are offered a way to befriend what is timeless and enduring. Often, when putting things together, we enter the pulse of a vital paradox: how small a part we are in the living Universe, and still, how our complete sincerity matters and contributes, the way one cell keeps the body going.

The question put to our daily lives, then, is: In love, in friendship, in seeking to learn and grow, in trying to understand ourselves, how often do we, like Kikakou, remove the wings of the thing before it has a chance to free us? We are taught at an early age to pull things apart in order to solve them, to break problems down to understand their parts. Yet in the terrain of spirit and relationship, in the sweet territory of compassion, we often need to *let things in* rather than break things down. So, the question each day becomes: When pressed by life, do I bridge or isolate? Do I reconnect the web of life and listen to its wisdom? Or do I make an island of every confusion as I try to solve its pain?

Often, the gift of surprise is what loosens our hold, moving us from dissecting things toward bridging them. Often, the unplanned and unexpected appearance of what is authentic jars us from our self-created sense of things into the larger order of life that we are all a part of. We repeatedly have this choice: to make all we encounter

self-referential or to bridge our small, troubled selves to the wonder
and mystery of the Universe and its life-sustaining vitality, which
like electricity is only released through the life of its connections.

When we can connect to what lives both at the heart of our
problems and at the heart of the problems of others, and listen to
those connections, we become bridges to each other, the world,
and to the spirit that informs everything. So, when we speak of
integrity, we are speaking of how we care for the tender bridge
between our innermost being and the common life of all beings.

Yet, being a human bridge—a living tool that puts things
together—is not easy. For everything from erosion to fear tries to
wear us down. But this is nothing new. Birds have always flown in
the face of gravity, and fish have always made their way to the bottom despite the buoyancy of the sea. It is simply part of our calling: to be a bridge, to lie down so that living things can join and
realize they are one. Kent Keith speaks to this simple calling in his
poem "Anyway":

> If you are kind, people
> may accuse you of selfish,
> ulterior motives;
> Be kind anyway . . .
>
> What you spend years building,
> someone could destroy overnight;
> Build anyway . . .
>
> The good you do today, people will
> Often forget tomorrow;
> Do good anyway.
>
> Give the world the best you have,
> and it may never be enough;
> Give the world the best you've got anyway.

> You see, in the final analysis,
> it is between you and God;
> It was never between you and them anyway.

Yet, when caught by the contradictions of life, we often forget there *is* a Whole, and we, like Kikakou, can be found pulling things apart. While this is understandable, this pulling apart can lead us to serve other gods. As the poet William Stafford says:

> If you don't know the kind of person I am
> and I don't know the kind of person you are
> a pattern that others made may prevail in the world
> and following the wrong god home we may miss our star.

Here Stafford implies that bridging is a practice by which we maintain our sense of who we are. It is a practice that renews our vitality, because bridging opens us to the energy, strength, and timeless perspective of the Universe. When we are blessed to remember this, our small but crucial role as a living being becomes clear. The great Chilean poet Pablo Neruda understood this deeply when he made this vow:

> So, drawn on by my destiny,
> I ceaselessly must listen to and keep
> the sea's lamenting in my awareness [ . . . ]
> So, through me freedom and the sea
> will make their answer to the shuttered heart.

Neruda makes it seem simple: By staying awake, we keep the larger truths alive. By staying on the journey, we become a living bridge that keeps everything living connected. Not only is our journey essential to us, but each of us is a stitch that keeps the fabric underneath everything whole. Yet we all know it isn't that easy.

It remains a struggle. This is one chief reason we need each other: to stay connected. How? By helping each other stay awake, stay true, and on the journey.

Someone who kept me awake was my grandmother. She, as I've mentioned, helped me understand the essence of the journey. The moment I'm thinking of is fifteen years ago, when my grandmother was ninety-four and dying. I believe she knew she was dying. I could tell because, time and again, when I'd visit her in Kingsbrook Medical Center in Brooklyn, she would sit on the edge of her bed and peer off into some distance she alone could see. Each time she did this, it taught me something else. This time, I had the feeling that she was imagining the other shore, the way she did when she was ten and crossing the Atlantic on a crowded steamship trudging through the waves.

Life for her was one endless immigration, one constant arrival in a new land. Perhaps this is why I am a poet, because immigration is in my blood. Perhaps this is why I understand the world of experience as one vast ocean we never stop crossing, even at death.

Being with her, especially near the end, led me to imagine the life of our spirit on earth as such an immigration: as one constant arrival in a new land. Given this, I've come to accept that, no matter the shore before us, the swell and toss of the sea never ends. When brought to the crest of a swell, we can see as far as eternity and the soul has its perspective, but when in the belly of those waves, we are, each of us, for the moment, lost. The life of the soul on earth has us bobbing on a raft of flesh in and out of our view of eternity, and the work of the inner pilgrim is to keep eternity in our heart and mind's eye when dropped in the belly of our days.

Even when we can't see it, there is a Oneness of things, and our call is to be a bridge between the infinite parts that constitute that Oneness. There is always freedom and the sea, always the shuttered heart that can follow the wrong god home, and we, in our humanness, always stretching between the two.

Some twenty years ago, I was traveling with a friend in northern England, through a small town called Oxenholme, near Windermere, when we came upon a bridge suspended in the fog. Suddenly I glimpsed the Whole. I felt safe, and the connections began to speak. I realized that we all take turns. We all have our chance to be a bridge between confusions, and we all have the chance to be brought out of our confusion by the bridge of another's love.

It was this simple glimpse of the Whole that stirred me to write:

*There is a bridge, that oldest of concepts, barely visible through the fog. It lets the water flow. The mind should be as hollow: letting the water flow.*

*There is a bridge that needs repair. Hear it creak. I drop many things, for what I carry overflows. If I lie down at one with the water, will you think me a bridge or obstacle? I need repair where I can't see.*

*There is a bridge, that oldest music which curls the heart. It lets the water flow. I drop many things, but the light ones fall like flowers or compliments or acceptance of new ideas. Drop something light for me or you or for the earth. We need much human rain.*

*There is a bridge at Oxenholme, I saw it through the fog, made from the path of swooping gulls, the same air swept and swept and swept, between us all, the same dream dropped, picked up again.*

# THE WORK OF LOVE

*They say that spirits make music*
*by moving through the breaks*
*in what is living.*

*If so, the work of love*
*is to hold each other and listen.*

When I was ill, it was easy to separate myself from others, as a patient surrounded by caregivers. While this, of course, was outwardly accurate, in the truer moments of crisis, we needed each other, and it was hard to tell who was ill and who was well, who was giving and who was getting. In the center of it, we just tumbled in an authentic embrace that saved us all.

During those days, I had a dream in which love was the fire and experience was the wood. And since, I've come to understand that it is the loving of experience that releases the warmth and light that waits in each of us. This is why experience is necessary, for living through it, the love we are born with becomes who we are.

My own time on earth has led me to believe in two powerful instruments that turn experience into love: holding and listening. For every time I have held or been held, every time I have listened or been listened to, experience burns like wood in that eternal fire, and I find myself in the presence of love. This has always been so.

Consider these two old beliefs that carry the wisdom and challenge of holding and listening.

The first is the age-old notion that when holding a shell to your ear, you can hear the ocean. It always seems to work. The scrutiny of medicine has revealed that when you hold that shell to your ear, you actually hear your own pulsations, the ocean of your blood being played back to you. Yet this fact does not diminish this mystery. It only enhances it. For holding a shell to our ear teaches us how to hear the Whole through the part, and how to find the Universe within us. It teaches us that when we dare to hold another being, like a shell, to our ear, we hear both the mystery of all life *and* the ocean of our own blood.

Amazingly, each being has the story of the Universe encoded within them. Each soul is a shell shaped by the currents of the deep. Even physically, the inner ear—that delicate source of balance—is shaped like a conch. And so, whatever is held and listened to will show us where it lives in the world and in us.

This brings us to the second belief: the folklore that if a horse breaks a leg, it must be put down. I've discovered that this isn't true. Oh it's true that it happens. Breeders shoot horses with broken legs, as if there's nothing to be done. But now I know they do this for themselves, not wanting to care for a horse that cannot run.

In just this way, fearful and selfish people cut the cord to those who are broken, not wanting to sit with a friend who can't find tomorrow, not wanting to be saddled with someone who will slow them down, not wanting to face what is broken in themselves. In this lies the challenge of compassion. For when we dare to hold those forced to the ground, dare to hold them close, the truth of holding and listening sings and we are carried into the wisdom of broken bones and how things heal.

These are quiet braveries we all need: The courage to wait and watch with all of who we are. The courage to admit that we are not alone. The courage to hold each other to the ear of our heart. And the courage to care for things that are broken.

The practice ground for these braveries is always the small things at hand. Somehow, through the practice of doing small things with great love, as Mother Teresa puts it, we learn how to be brave. In truth, the work of love is tending to small things *completely*. Such tending opens the mystery. By the large-heartedness of our smallest attention, we enter the ocean of love that carries us all.

Simply and profoundly, the work of love is to love. For in that act, the Universe comes alive. Such aliveness is the space that opens between us, as Martin Buber says, when two bow and touch in a true way.

# FAME AND PEACE

*I want to be famous in the way a pulley is famous,*
*Or a buttonhole, not because it did anything spectacular,*
*But because it never forgot what it could do.*

—NAOMI SHIHAB NYE

I was recently in San Francisco, softly playing an out-of-tune piano in a hotel lobby, waiting for a cab. I was meeting some friends for dinner at a restaurant on lower Mission Street. The cabbie ducked his head in the door, heard me playing, and muttered, "Hey, I need a piano player." As we sped through the hills, down Geary and past Van Ness, this innocent and weathered man-child began to tell me his dreams: "I'm goin' to New York, back to school, so I can sing on Broadway. I'm gonna do it. I promise you."

At first I receded, not wanting to get too drawn into his animated world, but he wasn't posing or strutting. I looked at his eyes in the rearview mirror. He was searching mine. No, this one was just a soft, spinning soul with nothing left between his feelings and the world. So I inquired and he said that he'd found his calling. He was meant to sing; in particular, he was captivated, obsessed, with *Beauty and the Beast.*

By now he was doing three things at once. He was trying to find the restaurant, trying to look at me through the mirror, and trying to hook up his CD player so he could sing along and show me his gift, his obsession. And there I was, spinning through the streets as this raw soul was singing the Beast's lament in the rearview mirror.

As he sped away, I realized that I'd been graced by a living image of what we all struggle with: wanting to have our humanity accepted while searching for a place to land. He was me. He was all of us. My God, we're all driving beat-up cabs, obsessed with *Beauty and the Beast,* just waiting for someone—anyone—to sing to. And though he thought he was after fame, like most of us, he was sorely after peace.

Like me. From an early age, I so wanted to make it, to be successful. It almost didn't matter at what. I think this came from a drive to achieve and the secret wish to get love from strangers, to make up for the estrangements of living in my home.

Of course, this quest for celebrity is one of our modern addictions. It's as if being seen and applauded will drown out the pain and confusion of our lives. It's hard to believe, but it takes courage and fortitude, and often sudden suffering, to accept that we are ordinary. And then it takes humility and openness to discover the wonder waiting there.

For me, in particular, it was the pierce of every breath after losing a rib that broke me of my search for fame. I found myself wanting less and less, until I wanted simply to breathe, to wake and watch the night turn to day. I found that pain had opened me to the music beneath the music.

You see, I had tried so hard to please that I never realized no one is watching. I imagined, like every child at school, that my parents were sitting just out of view like those quiet doctors behind clean mirrors. I even felt the future gather like an audience, ready to marvel at how much I had done with so little.

But when I woke bleeding after surgery, with all those white-coated angels breathing against me, I couldn't talk, and the audience was gone. I cried way inside and the sobs were no more than the water of a de-shelled spirit soaking ground.

Now years have passed, and I wait long hours in the sun to see the birch fall of its own weight into the lake. How it seems to punctuate God's mime. Nothing sad about it. And sometimes, at night, when the dog is asleep and the owl is beginning to stare into what no one ever sees, I stand on the deck and feel the black spill off the stars; feel it coat the earth, the trees, the minds of children half asleep; feel the stillness evaporate all notions of fame into the space that waits for light.

Now I understand that, despite our pressing busyness and endless worry, we need that stillness from which all things grow. Despite our distorted want to be the sun, we are more like plants growing toward the light. Despite our secret want to be in control, we need the armless surrender of a drop longing for the ocean.

# THE DRAMA
# OF OUR BLEEDING

*Somewhere*
*beneath his personality,*
*beneath his good will,*
*somewhere in the*
*chemistry of spirit*
*that enables flesh*
*to heal, he wanted*
*to close his eyes and*
*exhale the world,*
*doing his small*
*part to blunt*
*the edges.*

Like gravity, the presence and impact of suffering is an element of life we can't escape. It's interesting that the root of the word *suffer* means "to feel keenly." Immediately, we are faced with a paradox: While feeling keenly is what opens us to suffering, feeling keenly is also what opens us to beauty, love, and joy. One of the relentless mysteries of life is that you can't have one without the other. They are inseparable.

It's very much like the nature of water. We can't say, "I'd prefer the hydrogen only, please." Once you separate its elements, it is no longer water, no longer quenching. It is the same with joy and suffering. Together they form the water of life, and it is the gift of feeling keenly that allows us to drink from that source. Once we try to separate the joy from the sorrow, it is no longer life, no longer essential.

One of the great difficulties in our human journey is our struggle to withstand and penetrate the nature of this paradox. So often, we fall to one side or the other, spending much of our energy either trying to avoid our suffering or being trapped in it. When avoiding our suffering, we enter the colder realms of numbness and addiction. When trapped within the labyrinth of our pain, we are subject to reenact the tensions of our suffering over and over. In this struggle, not just to endure our suffering but to penetrate it, we can so easily slip from facing life and become sad actors in the drama of our bleeding, running from what pains us or constantly reliving it. For sure, we all experience both the avoidance and the reliving, yet, when blessed, we're able to drop below our pain and our avoidance of it, and briefly taste both the joy and the sorrow at once. Moments like this give us a glimpse of the underlying freshness from which all feelings get their power.

It was Carl Jung who said, "Neurosis is the substitute for legitimate suffering." What I think he means is that we tend to occupy ourselves with worrisome activities and preoccupations in order to divert ourselves from the necessary task of feeling what is ours alone to feel. Rather than feel our loneliness, we will run nakedly to strangers. Rather than feel the brunt of being abandoned, we will construct excuse after excuse to reframe the relationship. Rather than feel our sadness and disappointment, we will replay the event to ourselves and others like a film with no ending. It is this cultivation of neurosis and all its scripts that feeds the drama of our bleeding.

I used to spend so much time reframing the actions of others. A friend would not call and be less than a friend, would not show up or trample me in their need. One would gather me close, make things feel safe, then cut in the softer places. And I would tire myself making excuses for them, unwilling to accept that this is who they are. I so wanted the family I never had that all my energy and love went into painting the world with reasons. I now see that this has kept me from the truth of my self.

One of the surprising aftermaths of my illness was that many of those who helped me stay alive, who faced horrible things with me, distanced themselves once I was well and beginning a new life. I was stunned by this. I kept replaying my own film with no ending, refusing my own particular sorrow, until after one more telling, an older woman said, "While their love and courage during your illness is not to be denied, it is easier to show up when one is dying than when one is truly living."

We love to be distracted by the anticipation of catastrophe and the swell and arc of tragedy. It's easier than facing the risk of feeling keenly with nowhere to hide. I do not pretend to be a master at feeling keenly. I'm barely an apprentice. The tumbles of life have simply tossed me into the open, and dusting myself off, I can now see more clearly.

So all I can offer are stories and dreams. Here are two.

The first is the story of William Blake, a visionary thinker and artist, far ahead of his time. As an artist, he invented a new form of printmaking that reversed the standard process. No one knows for sure, but it appears he had two reasons for doing this. First, as a pioneer in combining his poems and paintings, he needed a means to more easily merge word and paint. Second, from a philosophical standpoint, he needed an artistic process more consistent with his view of life.

Before Blake, the chief process of printmaking, dating back to the Renaissance, was *intaglio* (Italian for *carving*). In this process, a design is cut into a copper plate and a print is pulled from ink held in the cut-out furrows. This process is consistent with the view that human beings are like blank slates inscribed by experience.

The shape and meaning of who we are is discovered or revealed by what happens to us, by the marks and cuts life leaves in us.

Blake reversed the process into *relief etching,* in which all the excess is carved or worn away and a print is then made from the ink that lines the raised edges that remain. This process reflects more closely Blake's notion of the human journey as one in which experience wears away all that is nonessential, revealing the Divine, already present in every person. Here, the shape and meaning of who we are is discovered or revealed by what is left standing once experience carves or wears away what is not lasting in us.

I've learned that the life of experience uses both gravities to shape us. We are carved in our humanness, the grooves of our wounds and joys holding a blood-ink that leaves a print of who we are. *And* we are eroded by experience of what is not essential, revealing the irrepressible edges of what has always been within each of us since birth.

I discovered this while standing in the Metropolitan Museum of Art, lost in Blake's originals. There, a woman, thin and hairless, stood quietly next to me. In the muted light, it was clear from the bluish pricks in her arms, and from the clear weight of her eyes, that she was in the midst of some cancer treatment. My heart instantly punctured, bringing me back to my own IV tracks. Then I returned to her. We seemed to follow each other through each of Blake's *Songs of Innocence and Experience,* each print hanging as a testament to what life can do to us. I could see the cut of her wounds in how she stood, yet I also saw a being, worn naked before me. I wanted to speak to her, but that part of my tongue had been worn away by my own journey. So I prayed in the muted light for both of us and watched her leave the sanctuary of those mad prints and disappear back into life.

The next is a story told to me by the wind. It was a month after my meeting with Blake and the woman in the museum. I was in our small garden behind the house when a voice in the wind swept through the hole in my heart. It made me dream that night of a thatch of berries I had to eat, berries nested in a crest of thorns. But they were the only food that mattered. And everything I'd been through, every path I'd tried, every love I'd lost, every friendship I'd fisted like a handle in a fire, every certainty that had crumbled into doubt—all of it said, *This is the only food. . . . There is no other way but to bury your face and eat of these berries. Of course, you'll scratch your cheeks. Of course, you'll bleed. But this is life.*

It made me realize that you can't separate the berries from the thorns that grow them, any more than you can separate the flowers of love from the prickers of loss that grow them. It made me realize that the precious moments of peace are incubated by crisis, the way the days are incubated by night. Mysteriously, the very nature and presence of God, ripe and luscious, waits like a berry to be eaten, a precious fruit ripening among the all-too-human thorns of fear.

# THE STRUGGLE
# TO BE REAL

*Enough chances*
*and the ego is effaced, a jagged tooth*
*rounded by experience.*
*This is how I know you now—*
*as something broken smooth.*
*We keep being refined by God's*
*friction known as the world.*

Falseness, no matter how clever, is brittle and thin, and is the first covering to be worn off by the storms of experience. We know what is real and true by what is left intact in us. This is why after crisis and suffering, we often know each other and ourselves so much better. During my cancer journey, I was surprised by how honest we all were with each other, more so than in the ordinary days that took us there. It wasn't until we were naked before death that I truly knew the beauty of those I loved. It was as if tomorrow waited underneath a waterfall that we had to pass through, and the force of that water was so strong that the only way we could survive it was to hold on to each other as we passed through. Once on the other side, we were squarely hosed down by life and everything false and extraneous was washed off us. Now it was our choice whether to cover ourselves again with things that didn't matter or to live more cleanly.

The struggle to be real can be a compelling teacher. And like it or not, it sometimes takes a great, raucous cleansing to open the chambers of the soul. Often, we mistake such cleansing for crisis or betrayal, for it often appears to us as suffering. But the truth is that God scours our infidelities of conscience the way floods rush ditches, and we are forced to tremble in aftermath, barely born.

Yet before we can uncover what this struggle to be real means, we need to answer the question "Where are we?" Not in a specific sense of time or place, but more in the sense of: What fundamental understanding do we carry, either consciously or unconsciously, about human life and its place in the Universe? For whether chosen or taught or imprinted by the pains of growing up, this understanding determines what we each *mean* by being real. And so our struggles will be different, depending on our starting point.

At the risk of oversimplifying history, I want to suggest that there are fundamentally two worldviews: one that emphasizes a belief in our connectedness, and one that accepts our disconnectedness and isolation.

As ancestors of connectedness, indigenous peoples around the globe, especially Native Americans, have believed for centuries that everything is related to everything else. All parts are connected to each other, as well as to the Whole. All parts are, in fact, empowered by actualizing this relatedness. Here, being real becomes a struggle to inhabit our relatedness to everything living.

Before the twentieth century, most philosophies offer basic variations of the fact that all living things, by virtue of being alive, have an innate vitality or life force that is empowered by the Whole of life, and that becoming fully human is the process by which we discover and inhabit our innate qualities of spirit and our relatedness to everything. Essentially, the East has pursued meaning by the apprehension of life through experience, while the West has pursued meaning by the understanding of life through the mind.

Then, in the rubble of a broken Europe, in the devastating wake of two world wars, an alternate worldview arises whose foundation is our disconnectedness and isolation. It is known as existentialism. Here, there is no unseeable web that connects everything. We are free-floating parts, colliding and reshaping each other, and the fact of our existence is all there is. Therefore, the only meaning that can be found or generated is in the moment we are about to enter and in a responsibility to each other. As we look at the history of the twentieth century, however, it seems clear that as the postwar world dressed itself in unbridled technologies, existentialism took a powerful hold on the profit-driven imagination of Westerners.

Being a mystic and a poet, I must confess my own bias. I believe in the sea of everything over the sea of nothing. I believe in connectedness and relatedness over isolation. In essence, a mystic can be described, simply, as anyone who believes that there is something larger than themselves.

You can see that, whether we believe in connectedness and relatedness or disconnectedness and isolation, each worldview will generate a different meaning of what it is to be real. A disconnected view puts a premium on individuality, on strengthening the will, on maximizing our separateness and uniqueness, on devising a morality that can negotiate the next moment as it rises in the midst of nothingness or chaos. This path depends on a Darwinian agility and survival of the fittest.

A mystical view, however, regardless of its tradition, emphasizes finding the Source of all relatedness, on strengthening connection, on maximizing our innate qualities of spirit and commonness, on devising a morality that honors the part in relationship to the Whole and to other living things. This path depends more on enlivening a web of connection that will allow the everlasting Source to sustain itself and us, the way blood circulates through the body.

The tensions of modern society become apparent as we drift between competition and cooperation, scarcity and abundance, and the effort to separate and the effort to integrate. Still, each of us is asked to discern our own sense of what it means to be here. This fundamental understanding will shape the struggles we devote ourselves to in order to be fully alive. So, if you haven't considered your fundamental position as a living thing in a living Universe, doing so will help greatly.

I want to share my own history with these energies. Often, when faced with the pain of emptiness and isolation, I have felt the urge or reflex to strengthen my will and individuality, to toughen my way in the world, to get more fit. I have often felt the oscillation between the sea of nothing and the sea of everything. And, to be honest, how I've responded, at different times in my life, has either intensified or relaxed my suffering.

It was cancer that forced me to break open, instead of just breaking and thickening my walls so as not to break again. It was almost dying that made me realize that the key to my survival depended more on strengthening my connections to all of life than on strengthening my individual will. It was almost dying that humbled me into understanding that, though I could gather more and more in the domain of the ten thousand things, such efforts muted my ultimate sense of connection and belonging to the Universal family, and my health suffered.

So, what does it mean to be real? I would suggest that it involves both an outer commitment and an inner commitment: an outer commitment to live as close to our experience as possible, and an inner commitment to keep our individual spirit aligned with the soul of the world; an outer commitment to stay transparent until what we experience is what we feel, and an inner commitment to stay transparent until who we are is joined to the source of life, the way a drop of rainwater joins the ocean. As well, to be real involves an acceptance of being cleansed of everything false and extraneous. Given this, how we go about lessening our isolation and increasing our connectedness, both outwardly and inwardly, is at the heart of our ongoing struggle to stay real. This alignment of inner and outer through the worn inlet of the self is the work of integrity. Thus, the spiritually practical questions become: How can we stay integral? How can we stay true and real and aligned? That is, how can we make a practice of wearing down what thickens around our mind and heart? Well, to start with, by being honest in our openness and direct in our empathy, we can minimize what stands between us and our experience of life. In actuality, living as close to our experience as possible is what it means to be authentic, and it is arduous, so we need each other to do so. This is the purpose of love and friendship and spiritual practice.

Ultimately, we all have this recurring choice of how to respond to the storms of experience: We can strengthen our will and isolate ourselves against the rough sea of emptiness, or we can strengthen our relatedness and enliven ourselves by feeling our way into the infinite sea that holds us all.

This reminds me of when Jesus led Peter to walk on the water with him. As long as he was devoted to his conversation with God, Peter was carried along. But once he became self-conscious, he began to lose his grasp of the Whole. It was then that he grew small and dense. And in his fear, he curled into himself and began to sink.

Every day, we get to choose between tucking and sinking or opening and being carried. Every day, we get to choose between despair and surrender. Every day, we walk into moments of emptiness and suffering in which we have the chance to try on our connectedness or our isolation until we create our own personal way: breaking down, by isolating and digging in, or breaking open, by connecting and taking a risk. I only know that, sometimes, when I thought I might drown in my pain, something else has opened, when I could take the risk to stay transparent and connected to everything I can't see. Then life's deeper current began to carry me.

So, where are you in this endless journey? Where are you in your struggle between isolation and relatedness, between nothing and everything? Where are you in your struggle to be real, your struggle to align your spirit with the soul of the world? Are you strengthening your will or your connections? Are you thickening your walls or making yourself transparent? Are you holding your breath or breathing your way through?

# THE CHANCE TO
# FORM INWARDLY

*As fruits are encased
till ripe, light comes
full term in the dark
and truth ripens in the heart.*

*The only way to know the truth
is to live through its casing of lies.*

A question we're never done with is: How can I discern what is real and what is distracting from what is real? With each circumstance or confusing situation, things appear muddy and stirred. So, we can act with urgency, guessing what's underneath all the agitation, or we can dare to wait until the water clears, until we can see what's at the bottom of it all. Of course, the press to respond prematurely is hugely distracting, and it often gets the better of us.

One of the hardest tasks during my illness was waiting for the crisis and fear and pain to settle enough, so I could see clearly what I had to do next. If not for the difficult blessing of waiting, I wouldn't be here. At first I was pressed to have brain surgery, but I waited and the tumor vanished. Then, after a tumorous rib in my back was removed, I was pressed to have aggressive chemo, which started to damage me, and so, despite the ulcers and neuropathy and the fear of recurrence, I had to wait for all this to settle until I

could see clearly that I had to stop. Each step of the way, I panicked and reacted too soon, only to be forced to wait until the
urgency cleared and I could see my way to staying alive. When
overcome with urgency, we tend to strike at life blindly. It's natural
enough. But, if lucky, we exhaust ourselves and then, doing nothing, we can see the waters go still and, finally, it becomes clear
what to do.

Waiting for situations to clear is a perennial challenge. Written
2,600 years ago, the ancient Tao asks: "Can you wait till the waters
of your mind settle?" Frustrating as it is, human beings have always
had to wait for things to become clear, and even then, the clarity is
all too fleeting. But authenticity takes time to rise in our blood.
Beauty takes time for us to fully see. It always takes longer to hear
with the heart, but the song heard there is lasting and precious.

Yes, being and becoming take time, and this commitment to
stay open is at the very core of what it means to be a person. *Person*,
from the Greek *per son*, means "the sound that passes through." As
well, the Blackfoot word for wind is *So Po*—"something going
through." These simple yet profound notions seem to name our
time on earth. For something is always going through—from
inner to outer, or the other way around. Like it or not, ready or
not, it is this constant passage of life through us that forms us
inwardly, if we give it the time.

No matter how we protest, life keeps coming, and we cannot
stop the invisible, imperfect river of time and its cleansings that
scour us into who we are. Underneath our particular cuts and disappointments at how the dream of life has unfolded, underneath
the way loneliness tastes to each of us, we are all formed by the
same unseeable force of life passing through. It is the passing
through of life that makes us a person.

If we don't take the time, we run the risk of arriving deformed.
There is an old story of a man who came across a butterfly half-
born from its cocoon. It seemed to be struggling and so, trying to

help, he gently exhaled his warm breath on it. Sure enough, his breath hastened its birth, but the butterfly fell to the ground, unable to fly. Its premature birth left its wings deformed. Our inward development can suffer the same fate, if we don't take the time to come full term.

Since speed and confidence are the traits of success we are taught to strive with, it takes added courage to welcome time and humility into our lives. Yet, without the openings that time and humility widen in us, the winds of life have no way to pass through and we stall our chance to become a true person.

It is no mistake of biology that rushing birth can have its costs. With the miracle of modern medicine, babies can be delivered prematurely when necessary. When complications arise, this often saves their lives. Still, some of these infants don't have the chance to form inwardly, and so they are born undeveloped: some deaf, some blind, some with cerebral palsy, some with diminished lungs. For them, their road in life is difficult and full of compensations from the start.

As psychological and spiritual beings, we, too, can suffer deeply, and sometimes drastically, if we don't have enough time to form inwardly. In our progress as spirits in the world, we need to give ourselves this precious, developmental time. Otherwise, we rush the birth of who we are and live undeveloped: deaf in one area, blind in another, unable to breathe fully. And so we, too, risk a life of compensation and inner disadvantage: straining to hear, straining to see, laboring to breathe.

The difference is that the life-threatening circumstances that necessitate premature delivery for babies do not apply to the development of our inwardness. We often push into life all by ourselves, never taking the time to internalize our experience. But the wonderful gift about matters of spirit is that, unlike physical birth, our conditions of inwardness can be renewed. We can begin again. At any time. In any way. For the chance to form inwardly and surface who we are never dies. Though we sometimes mute it, we can't extinguish it. Like the half-born butterfly, our colorful wings are always ready to unfold.

This reminds me of a woman who kept hiding her sadness in books, reading about other lives, as a way to deny the pain of her own story. This kept her undeveloped. Eventually she was in her quiet room, her small fire burning, another novel on her lap, and she couldn't read another word, because her eyes just wouldn't stop watering. She couldn't see the words, because her own untold river was overflowing the dam of her silence. It wasn't tears, she would later say, but the water of life finally rising into her days. Against her will, her need to form inwardly wouldn't go away. The water of life had cleansed her resistance and made her start again.

Our chance to be real often depends on whether we can stay open and present to time, whether we can let the urgent press of circumstance settle. Our chance to form inwardly, to become an authentic person, often depends on our willingness to let the winds of life shape us as they move on through. And sometimes, if we are blessed, life moves through us anyway, breaking all the pretty walls we've spent so long building.

# A SINCERE LIFE

Given sincerity, there will be enlightenment.

—*THE DOCTRINE OF THE MEAN*

As I get older, I value more and more the presence of sincerity, in myself and others. It is hard to describe, but I'm coming to believe that sincerity is the beginning of all generosity. It is how we make a home for everything within us and, in turn, such sincerity helps us find our home in the Universe.

My first experience of being sincere was listening to the sea as a boy. Its vast movement and mass wanted something from me and I had nothing else to give it but my awe, which it seemed to accept. That moment formed the pattern of my life as a poet. In truth, it describes fairly well my search for God. For in being sincere, the world has continued to open, not in superficial ways, but rather, the deeper nature of things tends to reveal itself when I am sincere enough to receive. In this way, sincerity is the opening of a deeper eye.

Since then, I've experienced sincerity as a way to enter the meadow of another's love where, in spite of our humanness, the garden of the timeless is still possible. Sincerity somehow invites a pause from the struggles we are so devoted to. It somehow opens the soft and silent place of awe. In people, it is first seen in the welcome of their eyes. In nature, it is the vibrancy felt in trees being trees, in mountains being mountains, in oceans being oceans. Whether in people or in nature, it is the unconditional invitation of sheer presence that gives us permission to know our own.

The ancient Chinese text quoted above, *The Doctrine of the Mean*, comforts us by saying, "Given sincerity, there will be enlightenment." To me, this affirms the quiet truth that only through that complete presence of welcome can we experience the strength and beauty of the Universe and the peace that connects all living things. Only through a sincere life can we know love and compassion. Only by devoting ourselves to sincerity can we know God.

But to understand the practice of sincerity, we need to look at the more human side of its challenge, which brings us to another definition of what it means to be sincere. If we trace the word itself, we return to Roman times, where the Western form of the word originated. It comes from the Latin *sin cere*, meaning "without wax." During the Italian Renaissance, sculptors were as plentiful as plumbers, and markets selling marble and other stones were as prevalent as hardware stores. Frequently, stone sellers would fill the cracks in flawed stones with wax and try to sell them as flawless. Thus, an honest stone seller became known as someone who was *sincere*—one who showed his stone without wax, cracks and all.

A sincere person, then, came to mean someone who is honest and open enough not to hide their flaws. This honest stance becomes even more important when we consider, as the priest and therapist John Malecki says, that "without vulnerability, there can be no transformation." I think he means that it is by and through our humanness that we grow and change and are allowed to transform. For without the places cracked and softened by experience and time, we remain too hard and fixed to be affected by life.

The Tibetans have a mythic belief that speaks to this. In Tibetan lore, a spiritual warrior—one who faces life on earth as a life of transformation—always has a broken heart, for it is through the crack that the eternal mysteries enter. When we fill the cracks, we not only misrepresent ourselves (for everyone has cracks), but we also shut down the possibility of contact with the eternal mysteries, and so, shut down the possibility of our own transformation.

My own experience with this is very telling. When young, it was my first fall from love. It broke me open the way lightning splits a tree. Then, years later, cancer broke me further. This time, it broke me wider, the way a flood carves the banks of a narrow stream. Then, having to leave a twenty-year marriage—this broke me the way wind shatters glass. Then, in Africa, it was the anonymous face of a schoolboy beginning his life. This broke me yet again. But this was like hot water melting soap. Each time, I tried to close what had been opened. It was a reflex, natural enough. But the lesson was, of course, the other way—in never closing again. It is, as the Sufi master Hazrat Inayat Khan says: "God breaks the heart again and again and again until it *stays* open."

So, after all the reading, after all the conversations, after all the therapy and spiritual seeking we can imagine, after all the hardships that life can have a stubborn soul repeat, the question becomes, as the Jungian analyst Russell Lockhart offers: "What does a relatively integrated and conscious ego do?"

Well, perhaps, once fully here, we are called to live a life of vulnerable welcome without hiding our very human flaws. To aspire to let the deeper nature of things enter our broken heart.

Still, being human, we are prone to distraction and denial and procrastination, and so, in addition to staying open, being sincere involves accepting that we will falter and need to course correct. Confucius speaks of this when he says: "*Making the will sincere* is allowing no self-deception."

A key element in making the will sincere, in correcting self-deception, is admitting our mistakes and owning what we do that hurts others. When we rationalize and minimize our actions, we are working the wax. In speaking to why Gandhi held such per-

sonal power in his nonviolent work in India, Martin Luther King
Jr. referred to Gandhi's ability to make his will sincere:

> If you ask people in India why is it that Mahatma Gandhi was
> able to do what he did in India, they will say they followed him
> because of his absolute sincerity. . . . Any time he made a mis-
> take, even in his personal life, or even a decision that he made in
> the independence struggle, he came out in public and said, "I
> made a mistake."

Sometimes we deceive ourselves and mitigate our sincerity
through good intentions. Often, when insecure and off-center, we
love in the way we want to be loved. Often, when caught in this
way of caring, we think we are answering the needs of others,
when in fact we are giving them what *we* would cry for, if we were
in their position. When more centered in ourselves, we tend to
truly ask and give what others need.

I first became aware of this when my father-in-law, a good-
hearted farmer, was watching his sister die. We were taking turns
sitting with her in her hospital room. He would come in frantic
and tense, especially in the evenings, and try to control our visits
around the clock. Finally, in a very tired moment, he blurted out to
me, "She must not die alone!"

Somehow, in that moment, I loved him more, and realized that
it was *he* who was terrified of dying alone. With all his heart, he
was giving her what he would want if he were dying. We never
really knew what his sister actually wanted.

This is a hard practice: making the will sincere and allowing no
self-deception. For sincerity is both the means and the end: both
the effort to own our frailties and mistakes when we stray from
what is true, and the effort to live in the presence of truth, whatever its form, wherever it is found.

Yet, how do we fuel this life without wax? It wasn't long ago that my friend Janet wrote me about her effort to stay sincere: "I think about the wood that keeps the inner fire burning . . . that certain wood burns longer . . . We choose what kind of wood we place into the inner fire, don't we . . . Some fires burn longer with only a small amount . . . It's the quality of the wood, how it has been seasoned, tended to, and how long it grew with care."

It's all about the life of care: caring for, caring with, and being an instrument of care. Again, we are not the first to struggle with these things. During the Tang Dynasty, Lu Yen, more commonly known as Ancestor Lu, declared:

Before practicing the art of immortality, first practice the art of humanity . . . [for] the Tao is entered by way of sincerity . . .

So, another way to understand this effort to be sincere is as a commitment to firsthand contact with the world with the goal of having nothing between inner and outer but the skin of our heart. Who we are, then, and what enlivens us rests on this immeasurable thinness called sincerity. And in order to grow useful—which is not always synonymous with being productive, but more about being a life-affirming agent—we somehow must discover our true place, not as instructed by others, but uncovered by the litmus of our own uncorrupted sincerity. As Rollo May asserts:

Anxiety comes from not being able to know the world you're in, not being able to orient yourself in your own existence.

I believe that the risk to be sincere will find us our place. By place I mean a state of being or mood of virtue, rather than a location or circumstance. The original sense of virtue, as spoken by Plotinus, is defined as "our tendency to unity." And so, the effort to live a sincere life can empower our tendency to unity. Such a life of caring can empower us to inhabit a place of virtue we could call spiritual *usefulness*: the kind of usefulness that humbles us into feeling both inconsequential and indispensable to the whole; the kind of understanding of purpose that has an old soldier drop his gun and stare into the sun with a sudden softness as he realizes his rightful place in the scheme of things.

# HOLDING NOTHING BACK

*My purpose,*
*at last,*
*to hold*
*nothing*
*back.*

*My goal:*
*to live*
*a thousand years,*
*not in succession,*
*but in every*
*breath.*

This was the lesson in dying and waking: to hold nothing back. To meet each moment with all of who I am. For who we are, when offered completely, fits the keyhole of silence that opens the door of the ordinary beyond which everything shimmers with an edge of realness that makes living quietly miraculous. And so I learned that holding nothing back unlocks the wonder and the soft underside of experience we briefly know as joy.

It was only through approaching death that I began to understand what living requires. And for me, almost dying was not like nearing a line and then darting back. For me, almost dying meant experiencing small amounts of death so deeply and rawly that the very elements of living and dying scoured my basic understanding of things. It was not a close call, but an unexpected, elemental taste of the DNA of life that changed everything. A lot like love and loss and the sudden appearance of truth.

As I look back, my first understanding of holding nothing back was as a teenager devoted to basketball. This holding nothing back pertains to sheer physical effort. It involves trying as hard as we can, giving our all, not caring how awkward we might look, or if we might fail. There was something vital about diving with complete abandon for a ball floating in midair just out of reach. It was my first visceral experience of exerting myself completely and having that effort turn into complete surrender.

And more than any sense of accomplishment, the great effort to immerse our complete energy and will into any one endeavor is a fundamental way to cross into the connection of all things. It's how the surfer paddles furiously until she catches the wave, and how the anxious worrier paddles through his torrent of thoughts until he catches the wave of silence that issues peace.

Stumbling further into life, I began to experience holding nothing back in another realm: that of the mind. This effort involves the life of secrets and questions, which when held in seem to fester and limit us, but when expressed allow us to feel the web of relation that is the nervous system of the Universe. This holding nothing back centers on the perpetual risk to break and reframe our ways of seeing and being in the world.

It reminds me of the wisdom offered in the Polynesian creation myth in which the Tahitian God, Ta'aora, sleeps in a shell, wakes, and standing, breaks the shell only to create the earth. Not long after, he sleeps and wakes again to find himself in yet another shell, and standing again, he breaks this shell, creating the moon. This continues until all of creation has been born.

It is the way the God within sleeps and wakes and stands in

each of us, repeatedly breaking what has encircled us in order to birth us into a larger experience of life. We all live this way: co-creating the world by birthing the God within. Like a series of cocoons, each phase of life has its own thinking that must be shed if we are to inhabit the fullness of spirit we are given. Interestingly, the shells once broken are not discarded, but transform into the geography of a larger Universe—only limiting and suffocating if we allow any one to become our entire world.

So often, though, we hold back: not wanting to wake, not wanting to stand, not wanting to break open the habit of our thinking in order to better know the world. Sometimes we become so attached to one form of self or shell that we live a hunched and suffocating existence, with no room to move. In this realm, holding nothing back means a willingness to say "I don't understand" or "The way I understand is no longer working." This involves a courage of openness to see things anew, to continually reframe our mental picture of things, keeping our worldview close to the pulse of what is authentic. One key to holding nothing back mentally is relaxing the habit of our seeing. This hinges on our willingness to voice secrets and engage our questions. For it is our secrets and questions that signal to us where our thinking is hardening and becoming confining.

One of the most difficult shells for me to break was that of meeting the world with a sense of ongoing crisis. Like many of us, I was schooled to carry around a suitcase passed down to me, only to be opened in case of emergency. I lugged it around for thirty-six years, and then, when being poked and prodded in the antechamber of the cancer world, I quietly and privately opened it. It was empty! And so the God in me stood and broke that shell, leaving my empty suitcase in the desert of waiting rooms. For the only way to survive the hegira back to health was to travel lightly.

Some inspiring examples of mentally holding nothing back have changed how we understand life. Consider Akhenaton, the

Egyptian pharoah who dared to believe in one common Source. He called that Source "the One Light" and developed a belief in the Sun as the living face of God. The belief in one God can be traced back to his courage in seeing a common element behind the many gods of his time. And Copernicus and Galileo dared to say we are not the center of the Universe—a struggle for humans to accept to this day. And Carl Jung bravely broke the shell of the individual psyche, to discover the sea of the collective unconscious in which we are all singular but connected waves.

In essence, holding-nothing-back-perceptually depends first on our willingness to accept that understanding-outside-our-shell is different from understanding-inside-our-shell, and then on our daring to know the difference. Holding-nothing-back-perceptually means expanding how we see. It leads to Einstein's notion that "you can't solve a problem by the thinking that created it."

Anoth[...] ng back involves the life of the heart. I sl[...] o realize that self-honesty and expression[...] d to eliminate the buildup that occurs bet[...] er life. Just as the buildup of plaque can [...] a heart attack, the buildup of emotional [...] of a healthy heart. The active and authen[...] aerobic that keeps our heart flowing clea[...] re here to live out loud!" Not loudly, just [...] we move through life holding our brea[...] with unexpressed feeling compromises our ability to know the world directly.

And most recently, I've begun to experience what holding nothing back means in the realm of spirit. As opposed to the complete effort of will in the realm of the body, this holding nothing back is a subtle interior effort of surrender that lets the fragrance of our being scent who we are, what we know, and how we move in the world. It involves the perpetual risk to know God in each moment, by putting down all agendas in order to be touched by a sanctity that is unrehearsed. In some ways, this is the hardest of shells to break and, perhaps, we can only do this for brief moments. But even so, these unrehearsed moments of being are enough. They can light up all the caves we've inherited and built on our own.

In my life, each instance of holding nothing back is a teacher. In the realm of the body, I keep learning how to give my all in order to land in a stream of grace. In the realm of the mind, I keep learning how to break the hardened province of my little world in order to humbly join the Universe. In the realm of the heart, I keep learning that perceiving and expressing is a sacred aerobic that keeps my emotional center healthy and clean. And in the realm of spirit, I keep learning that surrendering all my dreams and wounds and personal histories, no matter how briefly, allows the fragrance of my soul to renew my sense of life as an unrepeatable mystery. Together, these hints of grace replace the empty suitcase I used to carry. With them, I greet the world of others and the world of spirit through the continually breaking shell that is me.

# UNREHEARSED LIVING

*My whole life*
*I have tried to fly,*
*not realizing that our arms*
*are our wings, and we glide*
*by reaching out, and land*
*by reaching in.*

The Buddhist scholar Robert Thurman tells the story of a monk meditating arduously while a man nearby is kneeling as he rubs a tile in the floor. The rubbing grows irritating, but the monk tells himself that the rubbing is part of his meditation. Still, after several hours, the rubbing persists and the monk blurts out in frustration, "Why are you rubbing that tile?!"

Without looking up and without stopping, the kneeling man says, "I'm rubbing the tile into a mirror."

The monk blurts back, "You can't rub a tile into a mirror!"

And still rubbing, the kneeling man replies, "Any more than you can meditate your way into enlightenment."

This Buddhist parable implies that we can practice being clear, but we can't induce moments of clarity or know how they will draw us further into living. All the practice in the world can't instigate enlightenment or revelation. It can only make us ready vessels for when these moments occur.

In truth, practice implies practice for *something*, usually a ready-ing of the self in some fashion for the unexpected moment of life that calls once we're in the midst of it. Strangely, paradoxically, practice of anything prepares us for a moment that can't be pre-pared for. No matter how the heart readies itself for hurt or disap-pointment, we can't know how that hurt or disappointment will impact us. No matter how much we meditate or pray to open our hearts and minds in readiness for revelation, we can't know when such revelation will come or in what form of piercing or blessing. No matter how we work our minds to grasp the ungraspable, we can't know what subtle appearance of grace—what leaf or wind or dapple of light—will part our knotted ways like so many veils.

If we're not careful, practice can become a devout haven in which we mistakenly hide from life and all the unpredictable moments that carry what can transform us. Yet practice is essen-tial. It is a way to train the mind to be an open field, a way to train the heart to stay as clear and receiving as water. Still, practice only seems worthwhile when we can remember that it is no substitute for the moment of living.

One hazard of practice is that the devotion of *practicing for some-thing* can so heighten our expectations that we can miss the trea-sured moment when it comes. This brings to mind the story of a man who prayed every day to be of use, to be a saint, to be a man of compassion. In praying this way, he imagined repeatedly what being like a saint would look like. But every day, he felt no revela-tion or sense of understanding. He felt no presence of the Divine. He was saddened and frustrated that after all his efforts to be a good man, he was no closer to God than when he started.

This troubled man would rise from his daily prayers, waiting for some sign from God to lift him. And every day, nothing. Yet every day, he was always in the right place at the right time. An old woman would trip and he'd catch her and still he'd feel sad that he was of no use. Someone would spill a cup of tea near an infant and he'd block it with his robe and still he'd feel sad that he was not capable of action. His sudden smile would stop two sisters from quarreling and still he'd feel sad that he was not filled with compassion. A sparrow would light on his depressed shoulder and still he'd feel sad that he was not connected to nature.

This story says much about how we look everywhere for what is already within us, how we search for preconceived forms of God and love, while missing the actual rhythms of being kind and loving. The way flames dart about a wick, we often search for truth when it is the wick of truth that sparks the search.

I confess that the times I've fallen in love or tumbled into the moment have always been unplanned and unrehearsed. It's always been a matter of pulling some vibrant thread that is compelling. And, once pulled and followed, once leaned into, this vibrant moment opens to an all-encompassing atmosphere of Spirit—so close that I'm always astonished to have almost missed it. If I didn't dare to speak to you, or follow the blackbird's song, or stay in the overwhelming silence, God never would have appeared.

For sure, we may never rub the tile into a mirror or meditate our way into enlightenment, but we might be practiced and ready to open the window of our soul in order to be bathed by the sacredness in all things.

In real and tender ways, unrehearsed living means that we dare to let whatever floats or sinks or rises find its way to touch us, without pricking it with explanation, without dousing its pain. It means that we dare to make a cup of what we don't know and let the heart spill it. That, when spent and unsure, I can ask to be held and not regroup. Then, all this softness, all this yearning that makes the heart open like the throat of a baby bird, will deliver us into meaning.

When we can risk leaning into the unrehearsed sense of things, it becomes clear that this moment has never happened, is unrepeatable and miraculous. And in such an emergent light, when I

bring up what I keep inside before you, it becomes sacred and
scary, and you don't know if you want to touch or not, like reaching from a ladder into a nest of baby birds. It's too soft and sacrile-
gious, you say. It seems a place where human hands do not belong.
But I invite you anyway. Go on. This is who I am, who we are,
when no one's looking—incredulous hungry parts that, eventually,
if fed, will fly.

# THERE ARE TEACHERS
# EVERYWHERE

⁓

The Upaguru—*Hindu for the teacher*
*that is next to you at any moment.*

From the rotting tree felled by lightning to the water re-
smoothing after the whale dives down, everything is of equal
sanctity and grace. From the darkness we can't see through to the
tenderness of a grandfather afraid to speak, everything and everyone is a teacher. Each flower, each bird, each suffering, great and
small, each eroded stone and crack in that stone, each question rising from each crack—every aspect of life holds some insight that
can help us live. We can learn and deepen from anything anywhere.

Yet one of the paradoxes of being human is that no one can see
or comprehend all of it. Thus, each of us must discover the
teachers that speak to us, the ones *we* can hear. This seems to be
our job as initiates of being: to pursue our curiosity and passion
and suffering in an effort to uncover our teachers. Just as different
insects are drawn to certain flowers, though pollen is everywhere,
different souls are drawn to certain aspects of the living Universe,
though God is in everything.

While the geography of stars pulsing in the night may help you
discover the peace waiting in your soul, digging in the earth may
help your sister know where she belongs. And yet listening to elders

speak of their lives as they near death unlocks the things I need to learn. Each is equally a teacher, one no truer than the other. It's as if everything has to carry what is holy because each of us has only one set of ears and one set of feet to help us stumble on our way.

The moments that hold mystery, whether dressed in pain or wonder, wait to be treated with respect and sincerity, as if a message was carved in stone for you before you were born, and a storm has washed it ashore just in time, and you need all the help you can get to decipher its meaning. And we will be found by our teachers repeatedly—be they the moon, the thief, or the tiger—until we can uncover their meaning.

It makes a difference when we can look at experience as such a vastness. And the moments that open our lives become powerful stories in our own personal mythology, the retelling of which renews our vitality. For me, such moments include God emanating solitude through the waves of the sea, and Grandma staring into eternity at ninety-four when she thought no one was looking, and when I woke after surgery to the miracle of freshly squeezed juice.

So, who and what have been your teachers? What stories carry the teachings? And what inner history do they form? Who can you share this with? If no one, find someone. It's one of the few things that matter.

And where is your next teacher? In the loss about to happen that you won't be able to make sense of? Or in the stone in your shoe next month that has the imprint of a bird's wing?

It is all very humbling. For plan as we will, study as we may, search as we can, it is all a guess—a wild attempt to land ourselves in the open or in the dark until our teachers appear.

# MOVEMENT 2

*Steering Our*

*Way to Center*

# LIVING WITH THE SACRED

*A dog loves the world through its nose.*
*A fish through its gills.*
*A bat through its deep sense of blindness.*
*An eagle through its glide.*

*And a human life*
*through its spirit.*

If everything is sacred, then why does it feel at times so far away? Perhaps this is part of the human migration to and from what is vital. For the miracle of *what is* is never lacking. It doesn't swell or recede. It is we who, in our humanness, fall in and out of contact with it. When in touch, we are awake. When not, we are asleep or distracted or caught in the pain of living. When feeling the sacred, we are vital, even when in pain. When drifting from what matters, we feel drained of meaning.

Yet, though it seems elusive, the sacred is always near. All the spiritual traditions agree that the atom of the sacred is the moment. In this way, living with the sacred means opening ourselves to each moment, which animals are blessed to do without any effort. But for us, this requires the fortitude of listening, since as human beings we can be distracted so easily into making everything into our own image. It's how our ego misuses our awareness, trying to install itself as God.

I think I first became aware of the power of the moment as a child watching the wind when no one was looking. But it wasn't until I was crushed open to the moment by illness that I understood that all of life is waiting there. For years I had been seduced into *thinking* about life, as if it were the same thing as *entering* it.

Now it's all as simple and hard as this: Each moment is the entirety of life compressed in the experience at hand, the same way that each drop of water contains the entire ocean. Our job as human beings, then, is to be born again each instant and to die again each instant. For it seems that life is an endless series of births, deaths, and small resurrections through which we are renewed. Even more amazing is how the Universe itself is renewed by how we all live out this sacred cycle, the way that millions of cells die and replenish daily so that your body can go on.

The troublesome gift for humans is awareness: the thing that pulls us into what matters, but which if indulged too much will drain us of what matters. This has been known for a very long time. Some five thousand years ago in the story of Gilgamesh, we find Enkidu as a human raised by animals. His is a story of the tension between presence and awareness.

Before living with other people, he is completely free of memory and is blessed to be carried by each moment with very little consciousness. Governed by the moment in his animal state, Enkidu is fully present but incapable of both wisdom and fear. He might be clever in finding food and certainly can be startled by a larger animal, but he appears incapable of the deeper sense of these things. For wisdom here can be understood as a deep knowing of the web of life, while fear can be understood as an existential fear, the angst and press of emptiness misread as nothing. And both seem out of his reach. Yet as the story unfolds, Enkidu is brought into the world of humans and is befriended by Gilgamesh, the king. With this, he begins to know both wisdom and deep fear as his mind starts to work the essence of what he goes through *and* starts to echo on itself, replaying and re-analyzing events and concerns.

Enkidu's struggle portrays a life in need of awareness and a life plagued by awareness. From this ancient story, we can see that early in our history we knew that animals and infants share an Original Innocence through which they are blessed to know the sanctity of each moment. However, they are equally void of the awareness that can extract wisdom or deep knowing from their experience. Still, animals and babies are also free from dwelling in the opposite of such wisdom—deep fear or the angst and press of emptiness.

Yet somehow, even five thousand years ago, we also knew the burden of awareness and that humans as they grow drift into this paradox: The moment holds the secret of aliveness which our awareness can return us to, and yet our awareness, if not restrained, can pull us out of the moment and snuff our aliveness.

I experience this every time I feel something so tender I could break and talk about it too much. Each time I walk deep into the woods with my wife and dog, they fall silent before the mystery as I start to babble my words of praise, flattening out the mystery. And they just look at me.

So, for thousands of years, the human struggle has centered on: How do we access that Original Presence waiting in each moment? How do we nourish that animal innocence we know as babies without getting lost there? And how do we make good use of our awareness to keep us living squarely in the sanctity of each moment? I don't know the answers to these questions, but it seems each of us must find our way to participate in the birth and death and resurrection of each moment if we are to fully live.

As human animals, we have this mysterious consciousness to make good use of. If we don't, it just won't sit idle. No, it will run us. For awareness ignored or indulged, or used to avoid the experience of living, will take over our lives, pulling us out of the health of the sacred, making us sad watchers of the rain.

# STEERING OUR WAY
# TO CENTER

*A fish cannot drown in water.*
*A bird does not fall in air.*
*Each creature God made*
*must live in its own true nature.*

—MECHTILD

## DRIFTING AND STEERING

Though we can't see it, our life is carried in an open vessel that mystics have called the soul. Think of it as a canoe. Anyone who has been in a canoe or rowboat knows that if left alone, the boat will drift. In a stream or river, the current will carry us, but we need from time to time to paddle or row, to steer our way back to where the current is clear and strong.

This gives us a way to understand our journey on earth. For at the center of the stream of life is the unstoppable current of Spirit, the energy of Oneness, that vital Original Presence that all beings have longed for. Some call it the Tao. Others call it the Holy Spirit. Jung called it the Unconscious. Native Americans call it *Wakan-Tanka*, the Great Spirit. And Buddhists call it *Dharmakaya*, the stream of suchness. Whatever name you give it, it never stops rushing or carrying whatever dares to enter it. We only have to find our way to the center of its pull and our strength will seem to double, and the journey will seem easier.

This is the purpose of faith: to believe that this current is there even though we can't see it. And this is the purpose of will: to correct our inevitable drifting with a paddle here and a paddle there, not trying to do it all ourselves, but trying to restore our native position in the ancient and immediate current so it can carry us into tomorrow.

This image also gives us a way to understand our humanness and our need for inner practice. For when a canoe drifts left or right, or gets stuck in the roots of an old willow, it is not wrong or evil or lacking in character. It is just being a canoe. Likewise, our rush to judge ourselves and others for what goes wrong, or not as we planned, is a distraction from engaging the nature of living, which is drifting and steering.

With discernment but without judgment, the human journey is one of steering our way back to center over and over. So, this is really about learning the art of canoeing. What is the nature of life's current? What is the nature of the soul that carries us and how do we care for it? What is the nature of drifting? How do we learn the art of steering? In daily terms, how do we personalize our relationship with that sacred stream? In essence, like it or not, we are all small-boat builders and stream-journeyers, dreaming of the ease of fish while tiring our arms.

## A LIFE OF TRANSFORMATION

Fish are great teachers in two ways. First, all this drifting and steering, all this being battered about by life's current—it all transforms us as we go. And fish are great models of transformation. Consider how salmon transform their very biology during their lives.

They begin as freshwater fish searching through rivers and streams for a way to the sea. They seem to have an inborn call to find the deep and an innate knowing that they will have to transform their very nature to survive the deep, once they find it. And so, one day in midlife, the stream that's carried them opens to a sea and they, just in time, have transformed themselves into salt-water creatures that half-fall and half-dive into a deep they've always yearned for but never known.

Still, the transformation doesn't stop here. As they age, they need to leave the deep. They need to return to where they were born. And so they transform yet again back into freshwater breathers who swim upstream to lay their eggs—imbued now with the deep—and then they die.

We do not have fins, but arms that are always busy building oars. But the journey is the same. For life is a series of transformations and we, too, have our inborn call to know the deep. At each turn, we meet experience, drift and steer, and are lifted and worn by it all till very little remains between our heart and the world. This process can strengthen us or debilitate us, depending on whether our understanding of life is deepened along the way.

## THE NECESSARY ART

So, let's look more closely at how fish breathe. In this lies their second teaching. Somehow a simple fish inhales water and, mysteriously and miraculously, extracts the oxygen from the water. In doing this, it turns that water into the air by which it breathes. This ongoing inner transformation—the turning of water into air by extracting what is essential—this is sheer poetry!

For us, the heart is our gill and we must move forward into life, like simple fish, or we will die. And the mysterious yet vital way we turn experience into air, the way we extract what keeps us alive—this is the poetry of life that transcends any earthly discipline or craft or field. All this while the Universal Ground of Being we call Spirit is working its unknowable physics on us, eroding us to know that we are each other.

It is as the Mundaka Upanishad says:

As rivers flowing into the ocean find their final peace and their name and form disappear, the wise become free from name and form and enter into the radiance of the Supreme Spirit who is greater than all greatness. In truth, who knows God becomes God.

It is the drifting and steering along the way, and the turning of experience into that which keeps us alive—this is the necessary art by which we live and breathe. It is how we find our way.

# THE MYSTERY
# OF ENERGY

*I heard flutes in the wind*
*bending the uncut grass*
*and my heart seemed to split*
*as if something impatient*
*with my time on earth*
*was trying to lift me.*

There is energy in being alive, beautiful energy. Yet like all things that are essential and unseeable, this energy of life can lift us or batter us. Like small birds caught in a storm, how we open ourselves to the energy we experience is what saves us. Often, though, we are surprised by storms and, frightened, we tuck our wings and sink like a stone. I think the skill here, if there is one, is in sensing and learning how to ride the energies that sweep through us and about us.

I first learned about energy during my adolescence. I had a deep and early passion for basketball. I played in high school and college till I tore ligaments in my ankle. But along the way, I experienced two different forms of energy.

On the one hand, there was all that practice and focus and coaches preaching and instilling the notion that winning was everything, that stopping the others was paramount, that confronting those in our way required tenacity. This all spoke to a kind of *intensity* that arose from setting goals and negotiating obstacles. It engaged my attention for a long time.

But underneath all that was another kind of energy that fueled my love of the game. This was the magical feel of moving unplanned through the air. It was the indescribable feeling when the ball, from ten or fifteen or even twenty feet, might, by some stroke of grace, slip through the net so cleanly that the nylon cords would snap in a gentle way, then hang as if nothing had happened. It was how all the hours of practice let me lift in the air like some wingless bird for just a few seconds. This all spoke to a second kind of energy, a *luminosity* that arose from entering a moment of experience so completely that a lighter form of gravity took over.

The first kind of energy, intensity, seems to come from the press of complication. It is an energy of doing. At its best, it can let us know briefly what it's like for a fish to swim with the full power of the stream. It can also intoxicate us, sweeping us up in the need to figure things out. It can, if we're not careful, addict us to a life of crisis, in which we always look for the press of circumstance to let us know that we're alive.

The second kind of energy, luminosity, seems to come from the clearing of circumstance. It is an energy of being. At its best, it can land us in the subtle throb of existence that lines everything. If we're not careful, though, the want to clear things away can insulate us with an avoidance of the life we have to live. Here, under the guise of seeking peace, we can deny or sidestep our very real need to negotiate life.

It's as if intensity is the energy we are released into when juggling—all our senses tuned to one task. And luminosity is the energy we find ourselves in when all the tasks are done or undone—all our senses freed to simply listen.

There is no choosing one over the other. We attend these conditions of being and becoming so that we might better live with both. We attend these conditions so we might know when we are stuck in the pull of intensity, when it drives our lives, and when we are hiding in the cloud of luminosity, letting it keep us from engaging what is ours to engage.

Mysteriously, both intensity and luminosity, when entered fully and healthfully, can lead us to the same beautifully charged and vibrant place. For energy is the lifeblood of the Universe. It connects all living things the way blood connects all our organs. And just as no one organ can keep the blood for itself and live, no one person can "own" energy and survive. On the contrary, as the cleansing action of circulation, the continual movement of the body's blood through all the organs, keeps us alive, the cleansing action of the Universal life force, the repeated circulation of energy through everything living, keeps the Universe whole.

And so intensity, the energy of doing, is a form of Universal artery, pumping energy into things, while luminosity, the energy of being, is a form of Universal vein, drawing energy from all things. Both are necessary. Both are life-giving. One becomes the other. Both awaken and cleanse us.

# THE FACT OF
# OUR ONENESS

*That which can't be stolen*
*but only given,*
*that which survives*
*by opening us all . . .*

All the traditions speak of what Thomas Merton called a Hidden Wholeness, an unseen tissue that joins everything. It is in fact our deepest and oldest home. In truth, it is not really hidden, just so immense that it's hard for us to hold in view for very long. In actuality, the fact of our Oneness is constant and everywhere, a secret hidden in the open.

Amazingly, we arrive filled with this Oneness. At birth, there is no separation between us and other things, no subject and object. Of course, we must make this differentiation very soon in order to live. But inwardly, we then spend much of our time on earth finding our way back to that mysterious place where we were all part of one larger Self, all part of the same living organism, the Universe. Eventually, if blessed, we land where all saints and sages have always landed, back in the consciousness that joins everything, where there is no separation between living things.

Yet no matter how we stray or are thrown off course, we can, at any moment, regain our sense and experience of Oneness through anything authentic: an honest feeling, a truthful thought, the giving or receiving of a kindness, or any sudden surrender to the larger order. This is the purpose of love, of truth, of spiritual practice: to bring us to the lip of that sea where all things join.

The common beat of our Oneness is never far away. When we look closely enough at any area of knowledge, the Hidden Wholeness can be found. For instance, in nonlinear biodynamics there is a phenomenon known as coherence, which speaks to how harmony is as elemental as gravity. A Dutch scientist named Huygens first noticed this effect while sick in bed. He placed two pendulum clocks on his mantel and noticed that no matter how they were swinging when started, they would eventually begin swinging in identical motion. Eventually they would find their rhythm of oneness.

Even more telling is that if you place two living heart cells from different people in a petrie dish, they will in time find and maintain a third and common beat. This biological fact holds the secret of how all things relate. It is cellular proof of our Oneness. For beneath any resistance we might pose, there is in the very nature of life itself some essential joining force. Given the chance, we will find a common rhythm between us that is enlivening. Some suggest that this common rhythm is our home.

That we have this inborn ability to find and enliven that common beat is the miracle of love. For what are full hearts when excuses fall away, if not two cells finding the common pulse beneath everything? From Taoists to Christian mystics, our journey on earth is offered as a way to find that rhythm of Oneness and to swim with it and not against it. Brief as these moments may be, when we feel that common beat, we are vibrating in harmony with other life. Knowing this and feeling this can be a tremendous comfort and resource.

These moments teach us what it means to live in relationship to all of life. The great Native American elder Black Elk speaks to the power of our Oneness when he says:

Peace comes within the souls of beings when they realize their relationship, their Oneness, with the Universe and all its pow- ers, and when they realize that at the center of the Universe dwells the Great Spirit, and that this center is really everywhere, it is within each of us.

Albert Einstein affirms all this when he says:

A human being is a part of the whole, called by us "Universe," a part limited in time and space. . . . Our task must be to free our- selves . . . by widening our circle of compassion to embrace all living creatures and the whole of nature in its beauty.

Whether it is pendulums swinging on a mantel or heart cells beating in a petrie dish or strangers realizing they are intimates, there are indications of the Hidden Wholeness everywhere. Con- sider how a simple stone dropped in water sinks as it sends its ripples out from the center. Likewise, the deeper we are drawn into our common center—into the fact of our Oneness—the more we are compelled to ripple out our web of relationship.

In essence, we are here "to widen our circle of compassion" until we experience "that the center is everywhere." Whatever we attend to with sincerity is in some way a service to this end: to deepen and to reach out, and to live in that common beat.

# WE LIKE CHEETAHS

*The morning light sweeps a flock of birds*
*from the stone mountain before me,*
*all of us in an invisible wave*
*that perpetuates the beginning.*

Everything is changing *and* connected. And our call is to enter a dance with the things and forces of this world, not just deflecting what comes at us. For often, the things we need to learn are in the spaces in between.

The delicate way we are all connected cannot be overstated. The family therapist John Bradshaw uses the image of a mobile, saying that every family operates like a suspended sculpture of individual pieces tied together with string or wire. When one piece is touched or moved, the entire mobile shifts. Family dynamics are like this. Relational dynamics are like this. In truth, the family of existence is like this. Around the globe, what happens to one living thing impacts all living things. We are all suspended and connected in an intricate mobile called life.

A striking example of how subtle our connections are was reported recently in Africa. In unspoiled habitats where cheetahs have run wild for centuries, a seemingly innocuous grass has seeded itself in their path. During the last twenty-five years or so, the grass has cultivated itself into meadows of tall wheatlike stalks which sprout both small berries and thorns.

This small change has wreaked havoc as cheetahs running so free for hundreds of years are now scratching their eyes as they rush by the tall thorned grass. This small seed blown from some inner continental wind has inadvertently blinded an entire generation of cheetahs.

The particular lesson here is that the cheetahs didn't adapt. Darwin would say that over time these graceful animals will either: Grow longer legs to avoid the thorned grass. Change their migration path. In their blindness, go extinct. Or develop more resilient eyes to survive the cuts of life.

It is important to realize that in nature no one is to blame. The tall thorned grass is not evil and the cheetahs are not wrong. In our human case, when change becomes painful, we often distract ourselves with the blame game rather than adapt to the shifting nature of experience.

All this to say that we are called in this life to attend a changing landscape, both outwardly and inwardly. As emotional beasts, we often blind ourselves running cheetahlike into the thorns that sprout in our way. Sometimes this is unavoidable, but part of our dance as human beings is to live in full acceptance of the fact that nothing, not even the earth beneath our feet, is standing still. This acceptance gives rise to a sensibility akin to tai chi in which we can flow, whenever possible, like water around the thorns that sprout near our eyes.

So the deeper lesson is that adapting to the flow of life is more than reacting to things that just seem to happen. It requires our continual attention and movement with the life around us, the way underwater sea grass sways with the currents. For existence is a constant work in progress, not a still life, and like it or not, we are constant participants connected to everything in view or not.

In this way, there is an inner corollary to Darwin's insight. As the human spirit faces unexpected change, the human heart will either: Grow longer legs. Change its migration path. In its blindness, go extinct. Or develop more resilient eyes to survive the cuts of life.

Most life forms have little or no involvement in how they will evolve. As humans, we do. It's both a blessing and a burden to participate in how our children will be born and grow. Yet in our life now, we can only be aware and fully engaged. For nature will grow our legs or not. And perhaps our collective wisdom will change our path. And our stubbornness will surely blind us. But our devotion to life on earth just might give us or our children more resilient eyes.

# UNFOLDING
# IN THE WORLD

### Cain and Abel

*They secretly wanted the whole world*
*but falling, as we must, they found themselves*
*each with one berry in their weaker hand.*

*The more stubborn of the two could not*
*let go of his dream, and the berry seemed*
*so small compared to all he wanted.*
*The gap made him bitter.*

*The gentler of the two was shaken*
*into wondering if the dream had led him*
*to this berry and he was softened further*
*to sense the whole world*
*under its tiny skin.*

All things gestate and grow, and shed and grow. Many life forms do this more than once. Snakes shed their skin. Birds molt their feathers. Nests are built and broken down and built elsewhere. Most plants move through this cycle every year. As humans, we do this constantly in ourselves, in our families, and in our communities. We grow and shed and grow some more. We cycle through being and becoming.

This is a hard lifelong task, for the nature of becoming is a constant filming over of where we begin, while the nature of being is a constant erosion of what is not essential. We each live in the midst of this ongoing tension, growing tarnished or covered over, only to be worn back to that incorruptible spot of grace at our core.

All of nature lives this way, being covered over and then worn back to its Original Face. We, as humans, are constantly shaped by the two: the leaning into experience that we know as becoming and the cleansing action of being that removes what is not life-giving.

It is important not to overvalue either of these processes, any more than we would value walking over sitting. Often, we get distracted by trying to move from becoming to being or the other way around, when we have no choice but to live with both. Our most useful focus is to learn from what the two do to us.

But living in modern times adds a peculiar twist to this natural process. Our technology has so accelerated the process of becoming that it is more difficult for us as modern citizens to develop a constant and solid sense of being, let alone a healthy balance.

Consider the words *science* and *conscience*. *Science* comes from the Latin *scientia*, "to know," while *conscience* comes from the Latin *consciens*, "to know well." We could characterize the ability to know as retaining information and the ability to know things well as internalizing what matters. The impact of technology has extended dramatically what it is we know at a much faster rate than our ability to know things well. For to know things well requires time. But the advent of phone wires and the microchip have thrust us into a life of incredible speed, where we retain much more than we can internalize.

Let's pause a moment to remember Thomas Malthus, the British economist who predicted in 1798 that the population of humankind would increase geometrically while the food supply of the earth would increase arithmetically. He foresaw the problem of world hunger years before it moved into our global consciousness.

Now, if we ascribe the notions of Malthus to our science and our conscience, I believe the rate of our science, the things we know, increases geometrically; while the rate of our conscience, the things we know well, increases arithmetically. And the gap is *the human cost of progress.*

This is a very serious and subtle condition. As we retain more and internalize less, we lose certain vitalities. For example, since the advent of the camera and the airplane, the need to climb to see has been eliminated. I am not suggesting we relinquish these things, but something dear and essential is lost in our psycho-spiritual development if we no longer have to climb to see. Thus, the frontier for all modern pilgrims will be how to preserve those vital human efforts severed and tossed in that growing canyon between what we know and what we know well, between what we value and what we truly understand.

It is easy to see how this works on us physically. Before cars, elevators, and power tools, much of our day was physically demanding. There was no need for exercise or aerobics. Again, I would be the last to suggest we eliminate these amazing machines. But our need for exercise has not gone away. And just as we must jog now to compensate for the loss of physical movement in our days, we must develop an array of *inner aerobics* to compensate for the interior losses we are facing in modern life.

There are many examples. The calculator is one. It is a tool that I would miss. Yet clearly, an entire generation is losing the ability to calculate, to figure things out, to examine and imagine different combinations. Where do we get our practice at this? With the proliferation of television and the answering machine, we have gained enormous and immediate access to the world. But we have lost the capacity for face-to-face contact and the ability to immerse and focus ourselves deeply in one thing at a time.

This is not about condemning modernity, but recognizing that there is a downside to the gifts of progress which we need to attend, if we are to stay balanced and vital in how we unfold in the world. A social example of this is how we overorganize our activities. Consider Little League. Teams are preselected. Schedules are predetermined. Umpires are assigned. Then coaches micromanage nine-year-olds. They even signal them which pitch to swing at. While skills can be learned more quickly, a precious exploration of trial-and-error decision-making is taken away from these tender youths. In effect, their chance to discover how to self-organize is erased. There is something immensely healthy, if messy, that is lost when kids can't just choose up sides and problem-solve their experience without their fathers as umpires. Then we are puzzled when these children as adults are paralyzed in the face of what seem like ordinary decisions.

In our time on this earth, we are constantly bombarded with more to know and constantly faced with the challenge to slow things down in order to choose which of all this is essential to know well. At the end of each day, we are forced to ask: What is the one true thing of the many that we are shouted at to use?

In light of this, we might understand inner practice as a daily way to glimpse Oneness *and* as an inner aerobic to compensate for the human cost of progress. It doesn't matter what lineage or tradition such practice comes from, or if it is created in your own heart, as long as it is an authentic effort toward staying awake. Like breathing, it doesn't matter how you do it or what style you invoke, or whether you are skillful or awkward. It only matters that you find a way to breathe.

# GIVING AND GETTING
# ATTENTION

*We come, not knowing*
*that all the work is so much*
*busyness of mind; all*
*the worry, so much*
*busyness of heart.*

Being awake and staying awake depend on many things. We continually move in and out of wholeness and fragmentation, in and out of clarity and confusion, and in and out of a largeness of heart and a smallness of mind. When whole and clear and large of heart, we seem to be carried along, part of something larger. When fragmented and confused and small of mind, we seem to be tossed about, lost in ways we don't quite understand. And so we continually search for tools that will free us to be lifted by life's currents and not battered by them. One such tool is a frame of mind, an attitude by which we meet the world. It has to do with whether we are *giving attention* or *getting attention*.

Giving attention steers us back to center. It opens the vitality of the Universe and brings us back into the stream of Oneness. Giving attention is connective. On the other hand, getting attention is a form of drifting from center. If attention comes your way, well, enjoy, but cultivating it and seeking it is paddling away from center.

Getting attention is deceptively isolating. It ultimately leads to being seen but not held.

At the core of it, giving is often more crucial to our health than getting. It is important to clarify the difference between *getting* and *receiving*. For giving of any kind initiates the sacred dynamic of giving and receiving, in which the vibrancy of life circulates back and forth between us. When blessed, we fall into moments of loving where giving and receiving become one and the same. Getting, on the other hand, is an addictive, one-sided act by which we try to fill our emptiness by having life come to us.

Most of the time, giving attention is life-affirming. It's how we attend things. For inner health is often restored when we honor the need to recognize and verify. Somehow this validates our experience and connects us to the world. However, getting attention is how we are attended to. It seems our yearning for approval drives us to be recognized and verified. Here, being seen somehow relieves our angst about being insignificant, at least temporarily. You can see that these are abrasively opposite leanings.

For many of us, getting ahead centers on getting attention. Too often, once that place is secured, we are still getting, and no longer giving, and the whole process becomes self-defeating.

This is easily seen in any profession. Consider artists and politicians and doctors. In each case, there are those who feel pressed to stifle who they are in order to get to a place where they feel they can make a difference. But in doing what it takes to get ahead, the artist can lose the vision that giving attention first opened, and the politician can lose what calls her to lead, and the doctor can be hardened to what allows him to care.

In my own journey as a poet, it has always been a selfless attending of life that opens me to a wonder that still compels me to write it down, as a way to enter it further. But early on, feeling insecure, I was admonished by my own insatiable need to be seen, to get ahead as a published poet. Soon, the way an Olympic hopeful

does his laps, I was addictively going to the mailbox daily to withstand the faceless rejections, searching quietly and desperately for
the one small yes that would confirm that I existed—all this while
the wonder waited for my return.

Too often, once we're on our way, the momentum of getting
keeps us from giving, and we resurrect the wrong kind of power. It
can happen to anyone. This, I fear, is very true for some of us intent
on finding love. We become obsessed with getting attention to the
point that we develop manipulative power and not that deep, connective power. And once in a position to be loved, we continue to
take, abusing and weakening the thing that finally loves us. Again,
we must recognize that getting is not the same as receiving, but an
imbalanced, self-centered aberration of receiving.

The confusion between giving attention and getting attention
is so great that we often want to be well-known rather than well-
knowing. We often want to be great rather than true. We often
long for celebrity while secretly aching for something to celebrate.

So, when feeling the pain of being lost in your life, when alone
and out of touch with all that matters, give your attention to anything, quickly and fully, and the Universe, which has always been
near, will come rushing back to fill you.


## RENEWABLE RISKS

Yet how do we regain our giving frame of mind? How do we open
ourselves to love when we've lost our connection to everything?
How do we give when we've slipped into the pull of manipulative
power?

Well, when we fall out of clarity and authenticity, as we
inevitably will, there are renewable risks that can bring us back
into relationship with the life around us. These constant choices

to re-enter the stream of life are more plentiful than I can describe. And no matter how small they may seem, daring to take these ordinary risks will lead us away from being self-centered and back to being present and touchable, back to living and leading with our hearts. We can begin by looking at three such risks: the risk to see, the risk to attend, and the risk to be touched.

Consider the risk to see. The modern poet David Ignatow once said:

> I should be content
> to look at a mountain
> for what it is
> and not as a comment
> on my life.

Taking the risk to see is refreshing. It relaxes our lens of insecurity until we can see the world without us as its center. Only then will the world speak to us. Otherwise, it will quietly or noisily just mirror back our own needs and habits of insecurity; just as water will simply reflect our faces if we don't wait long enough to see through its ripples. For getting attention keeps us self-centered, and staying self-centered makes us seek mirrors in the world. And getting, selfing, and mirroring don't ever let us truly experience the world.

So, if we want to enter the realm of wonder that giving attention opens, we must withstand the tension necessary to see from below our self-centeredness, much like a diver who holds his breath in order to submerge below the surface. More often than not, the tension of seeing involves waiting for things to open up. Or, rather, waiting until we slow enough for our habits to soften and then *we* open up.

The Impressionist Monet was a brave example of this. During his time, there was great controversy over what his nonrepresentational landscapes meant. What was he symbolizing with all those colors shouting out their variations of light? Well, Monet, who seldom granted interviews, finally declared: *I am symbolizing nothing! This is what I see!*

Many thought Monet was making it up, imagining wildly what flowers and fields and large stones by the sea might look like if God held them closer. But what he did was much braver. Like a human microscope, he kept taking the risk to look closer and closer until he saw the warmth rise from the trees, until he saw the waves remake the sea.

He kept watching, after everyone else walked away, until he saw strange flowers break ground where only silence had been. He focused so far in that he, like Van Gogh, saw how everything shimmers. He proved by the strength of his attention that nothing can keep light out.

This is a quiet bravery we all need: the courage to wait and watch with a largeness of heart. But we don't have to be a great painter to see how everything shimmers. For the risk to see things freshly is always possible, if we dare to put aside our preconceptions.

Not surprisingly, when we can give our attention freely, and see from beneath our self-centeredness, the world begins to speak. Often, the risk to see quite naturally moves us through the risk to attend, the way beginning a step compels us to plant that foot ahead of us.

This is why when we slow enough to truly see the flowers or the dog or our lover, we are often stalled to feel them anew in all their beauty. It often seems as if the beauty of the world is hiding, when it is our seeking mirrors in everything that hides both beauty and truth. Rather, we are quietly asked to *be with things*—to see and attend them—until we can be touched by them.

Yet the trap of self-centeredness cannot be overemphasized. A blind French boy growing up in Paris during World War II was a profound soothsayer in this regard. His name was Jacques Lusseyran. He was an extraordinary man who went blind at the age of eight and who was sent to Buchenwald at the age of eighteen as one of the captured leaders of the French Resistance. His autobiography, *And There Was Light,* is one of the most extraordinary books I have ever read. It is why books are published at all. His inner experience of blindness is a testament to the existence of a spiritual world and serves as an example of the risk to attend.

In acclimating to his blindness, Jacques learned that we can seldom know the center until our self-centeredness is broken. Greed, it seems, is not restricted to the hoarding of belongings, but to the hoarding of attentions as well. Young Lusseyran understood this:

> All of us, whether we are blind or not, are terribly greedy. We want things only for ourselves. Even without realizing it, we want the Universe to be like us and give us all the room in it. But a blind child learns very quickly that this cannot be. He has to learn it, for every time he forgets that he is not alone in the world he strikes against an object, hurts himself and is called to order. But each time he remembers he is rewarded, for everything comes his way.

Lusseyran reveals to us an inner law of self and other. For each time we are blinded by our greed to have everything be like us, we forget that we are not alone in the world, and so strike against an object or person or circumstance.

It makes perfect sense. Our self-centeredness blinds us into thinking we can spin about without regard for the thousand things close at hand, and so we crash about, hurting ourselves and others. But when we can accept that we are not alone, freedom becomes more of a dance among the living.

It is from this place of inner understanding that Lusseyran made his way, once waking in his blindness to the fundamental way that all life is connected. In a spiritual sense, we can only hope for the same: that the losing of a lesser sight gives rise to a greater sight.

So, the aging painter going blind shows us how to wait and watch, and the young blind boy finding his way shows us how to attend to the world by admitting that we're not alone.

This brings us to the risk to be touched. For once seeing and attending, we are faced with the need to be vulnerable, so we can be changed by what we experience. Without this risk, the others are wasted. For without being touched by what comes our way, there is no chance of being winded by beauty or deepened by suffering. Without being touched, there is no chance to participate in the world.

There is an old fishing story from South America that shows how the risk to be touched keeps everything alive in a chain of events we seldom see. It tells of a small flower growing from a stone high above the worn paths that border the sea. The wind blows its subtle fragrance down shore, where a young woman is contemplating suicide, and something in the hint of flower lifts her for a moment out of her depression until she gets lost staring at the waves. The flower's scent is then picked up by a gull, who following it flies wildly through the only cloud in the lazy sky. Below, an old man in a fishing boat is stunned by the sudden appearance of a gull from a cloud. He relaxes his net and, underneath the shadow of the boat, the tangled angelfish squirm free.

To be enlivened and to belong are the gifts of giving and receiving, brought forth by the renewable risks that keep the world going.

# BEFRIENDING
# THE WHOLE

*When I live deep enough*
*there is only one direction.*

*When there, briefly,*
*the world overcomes me*
*and I feel a vibrancy in common*
*with all times and places.*

No matter whom the apprentice talked to, if she listened close enough and long enough, the words all went back to the same source, as if there were only one large thing speaking. No matter how many eyes she looked deeply into, they all eventually revealed the same shimmer, as if there were only one large thing seeing. No matter how many pains she soothed, the cries all sounded from the same human hurt, as if there were only one large thing feeling.

When she brought all this to her master, her master walked her in silence through the woods to a clearing where they sat on a fallen tree. The light was flooding through, covering everything. The master placed a stone in her one hand and a small flower in the other, and said, "Feel their warmth. See how both are covered differently with the same light. Now trace the light of each back to the sun."

The apprentice heard the one large thing speaking in the master's voice, saw the one large thing shimmer in the master's eyes, and even felt the same human hurt in the master's soft silence. The light grew even stronger and the master said, "We are all just small stones and little flowers yearning for the sun. What you have seen under words, behind many eyes, and beneath all cries is the One Direction."

We each carry both the master and apprentice inside. And, as day follows night, we take turns searching for what we think is missing and then feeling the presence of everything. Not just once, but repeatedly. In this regard, we need to befriend the one large thing so we can discover, again and again, that nothing is missing, the way the sun is not missing on a cloudy day. We need to befriend the one timeless thing so we can discover the presence that lives within time when we are clouded from what matters.

Yet how do we open the One Direction that waits beneath all our problems? How do we enter and honor our friendship with the Spirit that informs everything? Perhaps the easiest way to enter this conversation is to ask yourself to recall a time when you simply felt the presence of something larger than just you. Where did it come from? What did it feel like? Did it refresh you, stop you, disorient you?

For me, it was the sway of trees. When a boy, the trees would speak to me. They seemed to nod or bow as I would pass. I didn't take this as praise but as a quiet acknowledgment that I was kindred to some larger dance of life, larger than anyone had told me about. It never seemed that the wind bent the trees, but that the trees by bowing revealed the wind. I remember riding Greyhound buses across New York State back and forth to college and sinking in my seat, watching the trees nod along the way. And I felt at home in their hushed bow. They have remained a teacher all my life. For I have wandered into the entanglements of being human, forgetting about the larger kinship I am a part of, becoming tense and worried and fearful, and intent on one seemingly important thing after another. And then, when disappointed or exhausted or when the car breaks down and I am forced to pull over and stand off the road, there they are, waiting for me to stop. And they nod and I am brought back to what lives below my sense of self. They have taught me how to bend in silence. When I do, some wind behind me is released. Some call that wind Truth. Others call it Spirit. It is the Great Whisper That Calms that I always seem to find one more time than I lose.

When I lose it, I am troubled, frantic to be big. When I find it, or it finds me, I am humbled into the peace of being a small part of something indescribable. As we have seen, everyone struggles with this to and fro of spiritual clarity. As the child psychiatrist James Comer observes, "Much of the trouble we attribute to our young really stems from their sense of separation from the larger world."

This applies to us all. For much of our trouble comes from not being able to find our way back to the Great Whisper That Calms. Inevitably, experience throws us into the world. It invigorates and stretches us. It breaks us down. And if we can find our way, inner attention and love, which is the work of all practice, puts us back together. Such attention and love takes the pieces that are us and reintegrates who we are.

We are so small and the Universe so large, and yet we are carried. Not always as we'd like, but we are carried. Though we must struggle with feeling lost and suddenly found, with being broken and being put back together, though we spin like fish thrown in and out of our little inlets by the massive sea, the Universe carries us. As Rilke suggests:

Ah, we compute the years and divide them here and there and
stop and begin and hesitate between both. But how of one piece
is everything we encounter, how related one thing to the next,

how it gives birth to itself and grows up and is educated in its own nature, and all we basically have to do is to *be*, but simply, earnestly, the way the earth simply is and gives her consent to the seasons, to be as the earth, bright and dark and whole in space, not asking to rest upon anything other than the net of influences and forces in which the stars feel secure. . . . Ah, the knowledge will be there when it is needed.

This is our threshold to being carried: to simply be and to give our consent to the seasons of experience that will happen anyway, whether we consent or not. For life doesn't need our consent to sustain itself. But consenting lessens our suffering. So our challenge is to *be as the earth* and to surrender into *the net of influences* that holds everything together. When we can simply be and consent, then *the knowledge will be there*. We will find what we need.

This is as profound as it is difficult, and since we frequently hesitate to go thére willingly, we are often broken to it. And so we need as many reminders and doorways as we can conjure on the way. Each tradition has many such reminders. Let me tell you the story of one—the Spirit's Thread.

It seems that in the migrations of peoples across the earth, a tribe native to Siberia dispersed in different directions. One clan traveled south to settle in Japan, and another clan, crossing the Bering Straits, left settlers in Alaska and all along the western coast of North America, with the remaining members settling in the American Southwest. These native people became the Navajo, and deep in their traditions they are cousins to the native people of Japan. So it is not surprising that the Navajo and Japanese worldviews share a reverence for the larger landscape we live in. Both honor the net of influences that holds everything together.

The Navajo honor this connection in everything they do. Even when weaving rugs to lie on the earth, the Navajo worldview is present. For somewhere in each rug there is always a single thread that connects the inner weavings to the outer weavings. This affirms a spiritual law which says that if we are to know health, if we are to experience the mystery of being whole, if we are to know joy, there has to be a thread or inlet that allows what lives within *out* and which allows what lives without *in*. Indeed, only if in and out are allowed to inform each other can we live in the mystery and strength of the Great Spirit.

This is the Spirit's Thread, which love makes visible. It exists in everything. The thread of Spirit—there in the rock and the rose and the dark heart waiting to be known. And in order to befriend the Whole, in order to stay in relationship with all that is larger than us, we are invited to care for our Spirit's Thread. We are invited to honor the Spirit's Thread in everything, so the light hidden in the rock and the blood hidden in the rose might help revive our dark and waiting heart.

So, what does the Spirit's Thread mean, then, in a daily way? I think this beautiful notion implies that we are called to care for the small, thin thing that lives in each of us, that connects who we are to the world. We can understand that small passageway as our breath, our heart, or openness of mind. It is the vital tether by which we can tremble in awe at the infinite power and gentleness of life.

Whether it appears in a sudden shock of birds or in our lover's unexpected sigh or in a boy's sense of swaying trees, it seems that when we can name and honor the presence of the Whole, no matter how fleeting, such experience leads us to look for more of those affirmations. When we experience that mysterious unity enough, we start to sense a fabric of all that is larger than us. This invites us to surrender to the net of influences that holds everything together. Once realizing that we are part of this net, we often feel a growing need to stay connected to it. So, befriending the Whole involves an ever-increasing field of experience and awareness: The presence of something larger leads us to sense the net of influences that upholds the fabric of life, and sensing this net, we are led to develop and care for the Spirit's Thread, which keeps us connected to that living Whole.

Whether we consent to it or not, our time on earth draws us into an inner progression of feeling and awareness that, if honored, will enable us to know and benefit from a living friendship with the Universe. This friendship, if honored, will better equip us for living.

# PASSION AND DESIRE

*So much to understand.*
*So much to leave alone.*
*So much to do in this world.*
*So much to leave alone.*

*So many birds to hold*
*and look in the eye.*
*So many questions to ride.*

*As the ocean shapes a shell*
*by filling it and gushing*
*on, we are.*

Like many of us, I'm after that moment that opens up the world, that moment that keeps things whole: the sudden clearing in the forest, the swell of Mozart in my heart, the way time opens when my lover kisses me. And my burden has been to bemoan how it always goes: the sun does set, the music stops, the glow of love fades. Those of us captivated by the presence of all that is larger than us seek a way of being that will insure the recurrence of those moments. For some, it comes from the act of knowing. For others, from the act of caring. For me, it flares in the act of poetry, where, briefly, the knowing and caring fuse, as if soldered into something vital. As I get older, though, I'm coming to see that what I've known as the magic of poetry is really just the impulse to love.

Whatever our way, some of us long to be alive, which is different from just existing. This longing in us, which can't be extinguished, is the human difference. It's the thing we call passion. It can be a powerful instrument of renewal. It can bring us back to that Original Presence that all beings share.

It helps to distinguish between passion and desire. Passion can be understood as a spiritual longing, an inborn impulse for the part to rejoin the Whole. However, desire, as the Buddhists so wisely describe, is an endless yearning to have or possess that leaves us attached to things and people and places and even ideas. It fosters a clinging that can suffocate us. Of course, it's easy to see how we can confuse the two.

I so remember my first fall in love, her auburn hair and bottomless eyes. She opened something in me I hadn't fully known. And when she left, I had my first heartache and first deep confusion. Had she opened me to my passion, my inborn longing to be whole, which I now had to actualize through my relationships in the world? Or had she opened me to my desire, to this ripping emptiness that could only be quieted by having her love?

So often, in the living, the line between longing and desire blurs. Most of us are quietly searching for our passion. Some of us, especially when young, are unbound by the touch of others. Still others need to drown in music before they feel free. And some are ignited by climbing mountains. Others drive fast cars. Still others love to fix them.

Yet does it matter what we do: if I write or you read, or if you give or get therapy to re-enter that evasive sense of being alive? But what if you shoot squirrels or drink scotch or have nameless affairs or like to mope in a crowd? It does seem to matter how we get there. The history of addictions is the story of how humans fall darkly into what they hope will make them whole. So how we guide each other does make a difference.

Isn't this the goal of the artist, to retrieve access to that vibrant place and guide us through our visit there? Isn't this the purpose of therapy, to retrieve our sense of eternity and guide us through our confusing impulses along the way? Isn't this the call of artists and therapists and teachers and loved ones and the dearest of friends, to help us reawaken into Oneness, and to help us know the difference between longing and desire?

It is a daily concern. Just as we must choose between left and right, up and down, and in and out dozens of times a day, we must choose between passion and desire at every turn. For true longing will bring us closer to all that matters, while desire will stall us and divide us from our true nature. The heart when broken always has this choice: to cling to the idea of what broke it, or to long like trampled grass for the heat of the sun.

For sure, it is a difficult thing to discern. When we follow our passion, we keep the fire going. When we slip into desire, we are consumed by the fire. It is the difference between doing meaningful work and being a workaholic. The difference between immersion and obsession.

Before my cancer experience, I was thoroughly driven and consumed by the creative force that moved through me. It was a powerful if deceptive form of desire. I was eating myself up with a need for greatness that, like my first love, I thought I couldn't live without.

But humbled into surviving, I awoke, still here, and that drive was gone, nowhere to be found. Instead, I felt *drawn* to things. Not driven. It frightened me. I thought I'd lost my fire and I had. Slowly, I realized I had awakened into a more essential longing, a form of passion that has me attending a larger nameless fire that touches me and informs me, but which originates beyond just me. I have since found much peace and joy in this passion-born creativity.

Despite our endless struggles with desire, I remain amazed at how our spiritual longing enlivens our deepest nature by keeping us in relationship to ourselves, each other, and the Whole. Rather than playing want-and-have, we are humbled, if lucky, into giving until we are made whole.

It reminds me of two sisters living in a time very far from now. They both loved God. The one saw God in every fire and sea. Whenever near something essential and mysterious, she'd start to lean in, wanting to burn in each fire and drown in each sea. But her sister would pull her back, saying, "It's already in you." Though known by many names, the two sisters are everywhere we go: the one telling us to lean in and burn, the other pulling us back as she whispers, "You're already there."

# PRACTICING CHANGE

*The things that grow into soul,*
*though they depend on everything,*
*need no one's approval.*

There are age-old efforts that often return us to what matters. They include: the effort to keep looking, the effort to stay visible, the effort to stay committed to the moment, the effort to maintain our friendship with all that is eternal, and the effort to stop rehearsing our way through life.

Appearing hand in hand with these *efforts of return* are the dynamics of change that often invoke them. In effect, these dynamics of change are *struggle points of transformation* that can serve as thresholds for our passion, moving us closer to Wholeness. Or they can stall us in the painful traps of our desire. It all depends on how we negotiate them. In truth, facing the recurring dynamics of change is a practice unto itself.

There are many ways to describe these dynamics. Here is one way. The need to change presents itself because something in the way we are living no longer works. Our first challenge is: Do we hear it? Once hearing the need for change, do we accept it? Further still, do we resist it? Mostly, we do until the cost is too great. Even when accepting the need to change, there is the inner war of yes and no. And the Hamlet in each of us deliberates and deliberates. But how long do we weigh the costs? Finally, we are faced with the courage to do things differently, despite newness and fear, even if we don't know how. And then, once we try on the new, there is the courage to practice and integrate the change into the fabric of our lives. But, of course, by this time, or not long after, it can all happen again, as some other aspect of our way in the world goes obsolete. So we are called to stay open to this nagging and brilliant process again and again.

The transformational aspects of change seem to arise as unfinished spots in our journey where we can practice applying the deeper things we know well. When I resist the change I need, I try to invoke my commitment to look. When I seem to vanish in my old habits, I try to invoke my commitment to stay visible. When I struggle with the courage to try, I work on my commitment to the moment. When I don't know how to integrate what is new, I work on my friendship with all that is eternal. When the whole thing seems unbearable, I try to invoke my commitment to stop rehearsing my way through life.

When we ignore the dynamics of change, we end up lost in the rigor of old habits that once served us well but which have now become life-draining. A powerful example of this is the main character in the movie *The Deer Hunter*. Here we have a man whose almost paranoid alertness and lack of trust are the exact skills he needs to survive the jungles of Vietnam. But once home, he can't change and the very traits that were necessary for his survival in war prevent him from surviving peace. He can't adjust. And can't fit in. He sadly can find no love or comfort or sense of belonging anywhere. He is in exile with the rigors of his warrior self.

A more personal example of this comes from my cancer journey. Growing up, I became adept at fending off unexpected hurts, so that nothing would surprise me. Or at least, when hurt, it would never show. I became masterful at this. I fondly called it my catcher's mitt. I could spin and catch anything from any direction.

But once surviving, I realized that this reflex had the better of me and that very little could touch me, for that damn mitt intercepted everything. So I had to spend years putting my mitt down, undoing my reflex to protect myself, so that I could again be touched by life.

As you can see, no one is exempt from this process. So I ask you, in this moment: What is changing? What is confusing? What keeps coming up though you keep putting it down? What are you needing to attend but don't know how? What struggle is presenting itself and what effort of return is ready for you to use? Who can you talk to about the dynamics of living?

The value in considering all this is not to calibrate or preplan how we might react to change when we face it tomorrow. For being deliberate or methodical will not always help us negotiate life. However, if we can bring attention and focus to the ways we habitually relate to change, we can be sincere practitioners of what it means to be alive. Then, when faced with change, we might react more fluidly, the way a jazz musician practices scales so that when asked to improvise, he moves up and down the notes more naturally without any thought as to where the notes are. In this way, we are asked to trust that, like a serious musician, our practice will soak into us, so that we will engage change more deeply and more naturally when it comes upon us.

In actuality, each human being is an instrument striving to play their unique part in the larger Universal orchestra. And our longing to be whole and our suffering from trying refines us until, by being completely who we are, we assume our place in the larger ensemble of life. If there is a sense of destiny, it is less a predetermined role we each will live into, and more a gravity of being by which we, as living things, are destined to discover our vitality—by accepting our place in the mysterious Whole. Repeatedly, with each elegant measure of time, we are led into deeper ways of being through the counterpoints of change.

# THE NET OF
# INFLUENCES

*The beat under everything gives us
a life we don't know what to do with.*

We are not alone in this perennial task to be who we are and stay connected. For every spiritual path asserts a belief that everything is connected through a net of influences that each path names differently. And every tradition acknowledges that it is our human struggle to hold on to this fundamental connection. The Native Americans are wise teachers in this, in how they believe that all things are related. Thus, the native phrase *All My Relations* (from the Lakota *Mitakuye Oyasin*), which suggests that existence is a family of relationships, one influencing the other. So deep is this notion that when members of the Blackfoot tribe greet each other, they do not say, "How are you?" but "How are the connections?" or *"Tza Nee da Bee Wah?"* For how you are is embedded in your connections to everything that exists.

Black Elk puts it this way:

We regard all created beings as sacred and important, for everything has a *wochangi*, or influence, which can be given to us, through which we may gain a little more understanding if we are attentive.

*If we are attentive . . .* This seems to be the key. Our undivided attention opens the way. It turns "How are you?" into "How are your connections?"

So let's pause to consider what undivided attention means. I think it means more than just focusing on one thing, though this is where we must start. Our modern world insists that we multi-task constantly, tending many things at once, and while we are skilled enough to manage this, the deeper ways won't open unless we give them all of our attention. When we can fully attend one thing at a time, undivided attention takes on a deeper meaning.

Once fully present, beyond distraction, we are invited to enliven all of who we are until the things we keep inside meet the world. When we can do this, however briefly, the pulse of what is real is renewing. The sun reaches our dark corners. At this level, undivided attention is a *way opener.* It leads to tasting the influence, or *wochangi,* of the forces that surround us. It opens us to the net of influences. It opens us to the One Direction.

In the African Yoruba tradition, there is a deity known as Eshu—the way opener. He is regarded as the angel of experience. Whatever your tradition, isn't your undivided attention a face of Eshu, a living prayer that opens deeper ways?

Yet how do we translate this to our daily lives? How do we make spiritual things useful? Well, often, everything seems irksome until we are forced to take the time to surrender to what is near. Only when broken of our agendas and lists does the simple sanctity of life present itself. Only when shaken of our stubbornness does the deeper influence of things touch us.

Last summer, my wife, Susan, was away and I was asked to water an unexpected explosion of flowers in our yard. It took about thirty-five minutes to water everything daily. At first I sighed, feeling this was a chore. Then, as I dragged the hose around on the fourth or fifth day, the sun grew intense and I began to see the flowers individually in their various textures and colors.

I've always loved flowers, so it wasn't that I was oblivious to them, but now I was *relating* to them, *caring* for them, and this relating and caring opened a deeper, more comprehensive seeing. It opened me to their influence, their *wochangi* as Black Elk describes it. Now I could see that the dandelions had sturdy stems but delicate petals and so they required a cone of spray to quench their thirst. But the coreopsis would bend under anything but a mist. And the day lilies begged for a full shower. Now I marveled at how the different-colored petals would hold their drops of water in the sun.

By the second week, the iris seemed to lean into their watering. Though I began with much resistance, watering these flowers became a sacred practice for me, all because I was asked to give something near my undivided, complete attention. This chore became part of my Spirit's Thread. It pulled me sweetly into the shimmer of things.

Also, last summer, a friend of mine resisted all his usual distractions. For some reason, he didn't turn on the TV or the stereo. He let the bills sit for a while. He let all the burning news fit to print smolder. He even ignored his unease at not knowing what to do. And beyond his habit of tracking things with a skillful but divided attention, he became intoxicated with the stars: with the naked, impervious watch they keep over us, with the fact that the sky is not a ceiling, that there is nothing between us and these worlds of light burning as pinholes in the galaxies. It drew him into its magic and he began to read about the heavens and wondered if we appear as pulsing, tiny lights to them.

While watering the flowers so completely and watching the stars so intently, we both felt sensations of wonder and joy. It is beautifully so for many of us. What we tend to call hobbies are usually points of ordinary existence that we surrender our complete attention to, often by accident. And in so doing, we open our Spirit's Thread to the miracle of what is. In truth, most hobbies are sacred exercises in undivided attention through which we truly know the world. Yet we minimize these interests as extracurricular, when they are more essential than we imagine.

If we look at anything—a flower, a star, a spoon—long enough and completely enough, it gives way to a pulse of what matters that we can't do without. For it is the effort to be so present that lets us be who we are and stay connected. And it is both of these qualities that allows us to draw strength from the net of influences in which we are all related.

When we can honor this inner truth, we sing the very air into being, and hobbies become thresholds and chores become adventures and everything regains its capacity to surprise us. Then the world ceases to be divided into vocation and vacation or livelihood and hobby. Then the friction of living is made bearable, softened by wonder when we wake, and eased by peace when we sleep.

This simple call to attention returns to us like a mantra or rosary. It beckons us to *say what is* and to *hold what is*. It whispers strongly in our stubborn ear: If you find yourself struggling, depressed, confused, or simply bored, give yourself completely to whatever is before you. See it for the first time. Let it speak to you. It will not erase your struggle or remove you from your life, but chances are you'll be refreshed and the size of your problems will shrink more closely to what they actually are.

# NAKED ATTENTION

Somewhere in the heart of experience there is an order and a
coherence which might surprise us, if we were attentive
enough, loving enough, or patient enough. Will there be time?

—LAWRENCE DURRELL

When tripping into the heart of things, it is a full and bottomless attention with no intent or expectation of result that brings
us there. For me, it is often the experience of light, or music, or
the authentic stories of others that trips me out of myself. These
unexpected and repeatable gifts always bring me into a state of
naked attention in which I am opened to the sheer fact of being
here. Somehow, anything beautiful or true—*anything real*—brings
us in touch with that surprising coherence which defies ordinary
logic. Now I understand this moment of naked attention as the
tuning fork of being that lets me know that I am still alive and
able to be touched. Quite simply, it is through the beauty of
what is real that I trip from time to time into the well of being.
And in so doing, I experience a sensation of aliveness that defies all
words.

In truth, the very well of common being, the shimmer of relationship that lets us go there and return, the very place where love
and light become interchangeable, the powerful and lovely guide

of surprise—all these thresholds are inlets to the same mysterious pool. And only through such naked attention are we blessed to trip, by way of the ten thousand feelings, into the bare fact of being here.

My guide into such waiting and watching was an old farmer who spoke sparingly between his chores. Unknowingly, he became my teacher in my thirties. He was my father-in-law. One night in late fall, when the crisp air stilled the branches before the moon, he took me walking behind the cornfield. As was his way, he never announced where we were going or what we were doing. And I had learned not to ask.

Once beyond sight of the barn, he sat on a fallen tree and said, "We're owling." It took me a minute to understand that we were waiting in the night to sight owls. It was through these sudden and mostly silent adventures that he spoke to me, sharing secrets of the land that he'd treasured much of his life.

We sat there in the cold moonlight for a long time. Then he spoke, outlining the patience needed to sight an owl. As I listened, it seemed that some deeper voice was describing a way of life. It was this moonlight instruction that opened me to the mystery of naked attention.

It's been so many years and so many replayings of this instruction in my mind that I'm no longer sure what he actually said. For it seems that the words have been massaged by some attendant spirit who has translated their meaning for me. But here is how I remember it, the teaching I have carried from that night.

*You must venture out by yourself, must trudge slowly, careful not to disturb the things that beckon you. You must remain quiet and listen till your ears and eyes strain as one.*

*And then you must wait. Till there seems no life but the air you thought was wind. Must wait till the breath coming through you seems no longer yours.*

You must hold still, inside, must still your mind, for stillness outlasts lone-liness and great things that fly in the night will not stop for the lonely.

You must venture out till it seems in, alone, in silence, careful not to fall prey to your want for company or audience. You must venture beyond your hope to be thought of at all.

And there, just as everything seems nothing, as the night can't grow any colder, as the dark can't isolate you further, there, the sudden mass of feathers might appear above you, and you must hold very still, despite the cold heat clouding your heart.

You must hold that breath and stare directly in its eyes and it will spread its wings and stare back, so thoroughly, you will believe it sees all of what is hidden. And it may stare through you longer than you can stand.

And when it lifts its deep stamina, you might feel the knot in you soften and rise as if about to leave the world while the rest of you settles and roots a little further.

And then you will stay silent longer than you need to, not really wanting to return, unsure of what to say.

# THE GIFT OF SURPRISE

*When everything you've put off is here,*
*when every dream of love is on your lip,*
*when everything you've saved becomes a rose,*
*open your eyes, though they are busy seeing,*
*open your mind, though it won't stop planning,*
*open your heart, though it keeps remembering,*
*open and focus on the first thing you see.*

Our capacity for surprise is often an unused blessing. Brother David Steindl-Rast has described surprise as another name for God. With each appearance, it prods us to ask, *Beneath our problem-solving, what is life asking of us? Beneath our ideas of happiness or suffering, what does it really mean to live?*

So often, we seek to change things, only to find that our honest engagement with experience often changes us. In trying to make life fit our needs, our sense of need is often softened or broken until we fit life. Humbly, this inversion of intent is, in itself, a subtle wind of miracle. And surprise often announces that this miracle is near.

Because of the very nature of surprise, our first challenge is to stay open to the unexpected, not to harden into the position of our initial reactions. For this sort of stubbornness makes change a monster and makes learning next to impossible. We can't learn to see if we can't keep our eyes open. In just this way, staying open to the unexpected expands the openness of our heart.

## THE BUFFERS OF PERCEPTION

If we can enter this far, there is another challenge that we are faced with which is difficult for Westerners to accept. It is the risk to honor all levels of reality as *real*. So much of life is invisible, intangible, elusive, and still, powerfully impacting. Yet we tend, out of habit, to root ourselves only in the physical realm. Of course, this is our daily home. But as a bird's nest is soaked by rain and dried by wind and light, we are affected by more than just the twigs of our days.

So, yes, we live in the physical world, but it is constantly informed by the wind and rain and light of Spirit that we can't readily see. The Native American worldview is constructed to help its citizens remember this. One way it does this is to say, *We do not believe in metaphor. For metaphor blocks our being touched directly by the many faces of the Great Spirit.*

As Westerners, we say the wind is *like* God's voice. But the Native American says the wind *is* God's voice. We say water is *like* the earth's blood. But the Native American says water *is* the earth's blood. While metaphor has always been intended as a way to grasp and be touched by what remains unseeable, we have somehow over time inserted it as a buffer from the mystical dimensions of life that we can't quite understand or get rid of.

Through our will and self-control, we have buffered ourselves from other mysterious dimensions of Spirit as well. Consider how we often view memory. I had a memory of my dear grandmother the other day. She was laughing in her Brooklyn kitchen. It was so vivid. It was as if she had visited me. That's the catch. The buffer we create here is the "as if." As long as I assume that I call up the memory, I eliminate the powerful connection that she might have visited me.

When we assume that we author everything we experience, we snuff the possibility of being touched by the more numinous dimensions of reality. My sweet memory has a different import and quality of feeling when I remove the "as if," when I allow Grandma's spirit to have a life of its own. The truth is that I was missing her terribly, and she might have actually answered my loneliness, which I then dismissed as a private memory conjured out of my sadness like an old photo pulled out of my wallet.

Similarly, we dismiss dreams as things we make up, as fantastic exaggerations of our troubled days. Yet who knows? It is said that dreams are the language of God. So remove the "like," remove the "as if." They might just be X rays of our personal unconscious. Or glimpses of the spirit world. Or the shore where both meet. Dreams might be the trail of our unconscious connection to all beings—past, present, and even to those not yet born. When we dismiss them as only noise from our overworked minds, we go deaf to a subtle and sacred wind that is trying to steer us through our days.

Recently, in New Guinea, a poet accompanied an astronaut to a tribal gathering, and through translators, she was excited to introduce these natives, who had never seen a car or phone, to a man who had actually stepped foot on the moon. As it happened, the moon was full that night above the windful trees. Through words and gestures, it was conveyed that this man had been to the moon. To her surprise, there was no astonishment, but simply a recognition of kinship. Hurriedly, the natives retrieved one of their shamans, who conveyed to the poet and the astronaut that he, too, had been to the moon—through visions, through dream-walking. Humbly, the poet thought she had something marvelous to give to these people, only to discover that they had already been there. And the astronaut and the shaman sat under the night sky, comparing what they had seen on the moon, while the poet listened.

Our constant insistence that we are the self-creators of our own destiny, the builders of our own circumstance, can create a spiritual cataract that blocks us from being touched by the mystical light of spirit that so often surrounds us. As with the astronaut and the shaman, we often dismiss early wisdom traditions as primitive and infantile. Consider how we have minimized the Pagan and Hindu devotions to multiple deities as undeveloped theologies, when they are honoring how the Divine speaks directly through the things of this world. St. Francis would have welcomed the chance to worship Ganesh in the form of an elephant, or to pray to light as a divine source pouring through the hole in the roof of the Pantheon in Rome. Yet somehow we fear such direct contact with grace.

So a continual and deep risk for us, if we are to feel the presence and friendship of all there is, is to humbly lift the veils we drape ourselves in, the veils that insulate us as the self-creators of everything we experience. Whether we accept it or not, we are asked to let life, in all its unseeable elements, touch us.

How? We can begin by removing the buffers of perception that we create. *We can remove the "like" of metaphor,* letting the wind *be* God's voice. *We can remove the "as if" that surrounds old feeling,* letting that memory *be* a visitation. *We can remove the imagined sense of dream,* letting us feel our deep connection to other beings. *We can remove our condescending stamp of theology,* letting the spirit in all things touch us. *We can remove ourselves from the center,* letting the indwelling spirit pass through us, time and again, refreshing and rearranging us, until with D. H. Lawrence, we utter, without shame, "Not I, but the wind that blows through me."

## WHEREVER I GO

When I dare to ask, and when people feel safe enough to share their truth, I hear what lives beneath our buffers of perception. When I dare to listen, I hear story after story of the One Direction and of the net of influences by which the Great Spirit informs our lives.

Only last year, I heard a Navajo woman whisper, "When you dig in the earth, you can hear it moan." Is she imagining this or is she daring to be more open than the rest of us?

Only last year, an old woman in her kitchen in Tennessee told me of the time she heard her son call out for her in a muffled way, as if he were hurt in the yard. How this seemed impossible, as he was far away in Vietnam. How at that moment, as she found out later, he was so terrified in crossfire that he hit the jungle floor and called out her name. How she fell to her knees praying when she didn't see him in the yard.

And there was the Yaqui healer who had spent his whole life in the desert. Something made him want to travel halfway around the world to learn from the Maori Indians of New Zealand, a sea-faring people whose desert is the sea. For months, they listened to the desert healer ask, "How do we live near the deep?"

For months, they didn't reply. But finally, the night before he was to go home, they gave him an answer. In a holy offering, they blessed him with a bowl of fish eyes. He stared into the bowl repulsed, but it was clear that this was a sacred gesture offered to very few. They expected him to eat the bowl of eyes that had seen the deep that humans can't see.

So he ate the fish eyes and that night in the Maori dreamscape, he was carried armless through some clear depth where all he had to do was breathe and face forward. He woke knowing something of surrender and that—no matter where you live or what your tra-dition, no matter whether you obey or rebel—if you are to see with the eyes of the deep, you must take in what lives in the deep.

For no amount of talking or thinking or watching can substitute for taking in what lives below the surface.

Of course, our challenge is to know which of our experiences are old fish swimming, and to find the courage to eat the eyes of those experiences, believing that doing so will change how we see.

When the desert healer went to leave, the Maoris said farewell, reminding him that whenever he touched the skin of the sea, they would know each other's heart and he would be home. It is the same in all cultures around the world. When we dare to touch the skin of that sea that is deeply human, we quickly know each other's heart and are mysteriously home.

## THE GREAT OPENING

And then there was the son of a soldier who killed his own people. It was that gentle son who went in despair to his grandfather's bridge to ask in his solitude *why*. That night he dreamt that everyone who had been hurt and everyone who'd done the hurting met on that bridge. And in their awkwardness and pain, it began to rain flowers which, grazing their skin, opened their faces and they were healed. And the flowers, falling into the water, brought the fish who thought the petals were food. And the son of the soldier woke committed to the building of bridges and to the food of flowers raining from the sky.

In the light of day, this gentle son told me that the bridge where faces open is the Great Opening, the place where all things live and meet. When he left, I closed my eyes until that bridge appeared. It took quite some time. When I opened my eyes, I realized how small and deep one human life can be. I realized I can't possibly encounter everything, and so, it doesn't matter that I haven't experienced these things myself; that I've never been to New Zealand or dreamt of flowers raining from the sky.

It brings us to a crucial paradox of experience: While I can't truly know something until I've lived it, there is also a common source at center that is greater than all the experiences any one life can have. This is the bridge where faces open. At this threshold, we can become dangerously small and insular if we limit truth to just what our small lives have encountered. On the contrary, the true gift of firsthand experience is that through our breaking heart we can find our way to the heart of all experience. It is humility of this sort that can deepen our compassion, and such compassion allows us to embrace the underlying truth that all our experiences thread together to form the Living Universe.

So, though I may never be asked to eat a bowl of fish eyes, and though I might not have the courage to do so, even if asked, I can find the courage to admit all levels of reality into my heart. I can welcome surprise as the teacher that lets me see the blessing that waits beyond my small understanding of things. I can feel my way like a blind man, praising the existence of light because I can feel its warmth all over my face.

# THE LIFE OF EXPRESSION

*What is not ex-pressed is de-pressed.*

The cultural anthropologist Angeles Arrien tells us that throats and bones are the oldest instruments we have. We have always voiced and drummed our pain and joy. In truth, the need to express who we are is archetypal; that is, both necessary and time-less. And expressing who we are is less about describing ourselves than it is about letting who we are out in a regular rhythm that is as imperative as breathing. It is this exchange or flow of who we are—in and out—that keeps us connected to all that is living. Just as we must inhale and exhale hundreds of times a day, we must feel and express constantly. When out of balance, we suffer. When feeling and perceiving only, when only taking in, we are ripe to explode or carry the terrible weight of never letting anything out. For what is not ex-pressed is de-pressed. Yet when expressing only, when only letting out, we expend ourselves completely and, with nothing to replenish us, we run the danger of collapsing in on ourselves.

Ultimately, expressing who we are has a physics all its own. More than being understood, it is about not hiding our basic nature. Essentially, the life of expression is the ongoing journey of how we heal each other. And so, the importance of storytelling, for by telling our stories and listening to the stories of others, we let out who we are and find ourselves in each other, and find that we are more together than alone.

## STORYTELLING

Stories are medicine, small doses of what matters, and it is the telling that releases the medicine, the telling that soothes our pain and shares our joy. That the deepest stories are passed from generation to generation is a kind of cultural vaccine that requires each of us to ingest the ounce of truth each story carries. How? By telling each story for ourselves. It is in the truth of stories that we meet and join.

Inevitably, we tell and retell our stories until we understand all that they have to teach us. We tell and retell the stories we hear because we can't experience everything by ourselves. We keep stories alive because to re-member is to put broken pieces back together. We keep learning from stories how to make things whole.

It is not by accident that Native American medicine men put these questions to the sick who are brought to them: When was the last time you sang? When was the last time you danced? When was the last time you told your story? When was the last time you listened to the stories of others? It has always been clear that the life of our expression and the life of our stories are connected to our health.

In the Cherokee Nation, shamans carry story pouches filled with symbols that hold the teachings and heritage of their tribe. It is the holding of these symbols and retelling of their stories that pass on the Cherokee heritage to the next generation. Essentially, this is how every community passes on the struggles and paradoxes and lessons of living—through its stories, as an inner curriculum to those coming next. No one can live for us, but we can learn by the attempts of others. This is the true and useful meaning of heritage.

I was amazed to learn that in the Potlach tribe indigenous to the Northwest, they have one word for *sing* and *cry*. Imagine that when we unfold our suffering and our joy far enough, they have the same prehensile root. Imagine that all we express starts with one common, sacred utterance.

After drifting with this thought for quite some time, I fell asleep and had a dream in which I was offered this story that I believe has been dreamt before:

*It happens quite unexpectedly on an ordinary morning. Everyone, at the same time, shouts out the one word that voices their pain or their joy. At first it is a huge noise, as every pain and every joy is different. But as the words pull open the voices that speak them, the voices spill the ounce of being that all spirits share, and the cries of wonder and cries of pain begin to merge. Unexpectedly, they form one tone, and a single word shimmers, though it can be found in no language. Yet this shimmering tone is so familiar, it seems the ground of every language. And this word that can't be found is carried on the wind until it opens a silence that lifts the heads of those afraid of tomorrow.*

I am not sure what such a story-dream-message means. But it has helped me listen to everyone, intimates and strangers alike, as the co-tellers of a story we have yet to live. For you are my medicine. And I am yours. We are members of a broken whole. So, tell and I will listen. And we will heal. A stitch, a song, a cry at a time.

## SONG IS NOT A LUXURY

There is another deep lesson I have learned about the place of voice and song in our lives. I spoke of it earlier. It came to me in the winter of 1998, while in South Africa. It was there that I first came to understand that there is a wind that keeps blowing since the beginning, and in every language ever spoken, it continues to whisper to all who will listen, *You must meet the outer world with your inner world or existence will crush you.*

The South African people are an inspired example of this. They demonstrate, once again, in the history of human affairs, that when being true to who we are, we can more than endure. Most of all, the people of Africa sweetly prove with their irrepressible spirit that song is not a luxury but a necessary way of being in the world, a way of keeping the soul anchored in hard time, a way for each of us to experience the fullness of life, no matter what difficulties we may wake in.

Being with the people of South Africa, it became very clear that giving voice to what is inner is essential to surviving what is outer. I saw it in the faces of schoolchildren in Mannenberg singing behind barbed wire, there to protect them from the drug gangs. I saw it in the worn prison on Robben Island now turned into a museum to educate the young. I saw it in boys and girls singing for hours on shanty corners in the townships of Cape Town, singing to soften the harshness of their world. No matter where we live or who we love, no matter what we want or what we can't have, giving voice to what is inner in order to survive what is outer is the lesson I can't repeat or learn enough.

Upon my return, I wrote the following:

*I come to you from a land where elders have shown their grandchildren how to sing their way through. I come to you from a land where skin pounds skin. From the outside in, we call this brutality. From the inside out, we call this song. The gift of Africa tells us that song is the only thing that can outlast brutality. Whether you suffer an unjust system or an oppressive father, whether you have been in a prison of another's making or in a cage of your own construction, this sun-baked continent that carries the tremor of the beginning tells any who will listen that song is the only thing that can outlast brutality. The drums, if they can be leaned into, will carry you along. The drums, which have no beginning or end, will circle you through the many faces of pain and joy. And the drums of Africa sound the heartbeat of God, clear and unending. Even when oppressed to the point of silence, the drumbeat cannot be silenced. Even if you are born a funé, a storyteller who is not permitted to sing, there is song in how you raise your eyes to the unwatched sky. Even if you are forbidden to cry your truth, there is the Geuca Solo, the dance without words before the twice-locked gates. Pain held in is pain. Pain let out is dance. Worry held in is worry. Worry let out is the cry of a bird that lives on the branch of heart that no one sees. Sorrow held in is sorrow. But sorrow let out is the song of the continents moving together. Even if you are forbidden to cry your truth, there is still the dance without words before the twice-locked gates. No matter if the gates are generations old, no matter if the gates are in your mind, no matter if when you move, you stumble. It is the gift of Africa for the children of the earth: God is the wood of the drums, drums sound the heartbeat of the living, song is the thing that will outlast brutality.*

It has been six years since I went to Africa, and nowhere have I seen the inner life brought so vibrantly and joyously to meet the hardships of this earth. Nowhere have I seen the one song that we are all born with rise so fully in the throats of children. We struggle in our civilized world to stay real in the face of so many sophistications. But there, the children sing, unrehearsed except by their pain and their wonder. There, the children sing, unrehearsed except by the long wait for freedom. There, the children sing and plant their feet. They sing to the sky and plant their pain in the earth. Again and again, song to the sky, pain to the earth, until the rhythm of Africa cannot be denied.

I had been touched so often and so deeply during my time there that I was pried open beyond all protection until the one song-cry of life moved me to tears. The eyes of these African children are still with me. From shanty street corners to barb-wired schoolyards, I watched them enlarge their sense of self to survive the pains of living. And I have carried this teaching everywhere.

If I close my eyes and sing, though I don't know what song may come, I can feel the pulse of the world, both its joy and its suffering, as I discovered it in the low African sky. If humbled and lucky enough, we find each other there, no matter our country of birth, no matter the gates we find ourselves behind. And if we dare to meet the outer world with our inner world, we will surface the song that carries life, though we don't know how to sing. Like the children of Africa, we have no choice but to rely on song to stop the pain, the way that fire stalls the cold.

# FALLING DOWN AND
# GETTING UP

*Where you stumble and fall,*
*there you discover gold.*

—JOSEPH CAMPBELL

When medieval monks were asked how they practiced their faith, they would often reply, "By falling down and getting up." And there you have the whole muddled mess of being human. Over and over, this very humbling sequence returns us to the earth, to the humus, to the soil. Try as we will to escape or transcend the imperfection of being a spirit on earth, it is through this wonderful friction that we come to know God.

How we think about this matters. For falling down is not about failure, but about experiencing as many of life's positions as possible. It is how we learn. And getting up is not about vanquishing or conquering an opponent or circumstance, but about not getting stuck in one of life's innumerable valleys. The truth is that we can't avoid falling down and getting up, any more than we can avoid forgetting and remembering. It is how we integrate, one experience at a time, our human with our being.

Falling down is frequently an opportunity for transformation. As Rob Lehman suggests, falling down and getting up is our way of becoming conscious. It is how we aim and miss and lean into the difference. Too often, we are distracted by a self-loathing of that difference, of the gap between what we want and who we are. We regret not being perfect and this painfully stalls us. Yet each time we aim and miss, each time we fall down and get up, it is the plunge and reach of a swimmer's stroke that moves us through the water. There is no other way to swim.

Still, we distract ourselves terribly with the blame game. For sure, there are many ways to fall down, but it only inflames our petty nature to keep score as to who trips us or pushes us. This only cultivates a victim's worldview. Rather, it helps to understand the different ways we are apt to fall, in the same way we might understand the conditions of geology, so we can know the faults and schisms of this life.

## SAUL

As long as stories have been told, the fall that changes everything has been embedded in our myths as a riddle to be experienced more than solved. Consider how Saul of Tarsus, the soldier hunting early followers of Jesus, was knocked from his horse, how from his knees he was forced to see with the eyes of the hunted. This is told as a spirit-induced fall from which Saul rose transformed into St. Paul. As an archetype, we are shown that following any one idea or bias in a fanatical way will humble us, if we're blessed to be knocked from our horse, into embracing the very thing we oppose. This sort of God-induced falling down can save us from our want to destroy what we think we are not. It can save us by thrusting us into understanding that we are all, at heart, the same.

## ROBERT

More recently, my dear friend Robert told me about a self-induced fall. It was a snowy night and Robert was recalling the time two springs ago when he was determined to paint the family room. Up early, he was out the door, to the hardware store gathering the gallons of red, the wooden mixing sticks, the drop cloths, and the one-time brushes that always harden, no matter what you soak them in.

Back home, he mixed the paint outside and waddled to the door with a gallon in each hand, the drop cloth under his arm, and a wide brush in his mouth. He began to chuckle in telling what happened: "I teetered there for minutes, trying to open the door, not wanting to put anything down. I was so stubborn. I had the door almost open when I lost my grip, stumbled backwards, and wound up on the ground, red gallons all over me."

At this point, he laughed at himself, as he has done many times, and we watched the snow fall in silence. I thought of his little story the whole way home. Amazingly, we all do this, whether with groceries or paint or with the stories we feel determined to share. We do this with our love, with our sense of truth, even with our pain. It's such a simple thing, but in a moment of ego we refuse to put down what we carry in order to open the door. Time and time again, we are offered the chance to truly learn this: We cannot hold on to things and enter. We must put down what we carry, open the door, and then take up only what we need to bring inside.

It is a basic human sequence: gather, prepare, put down, enter. But failing as we do, we always have that second chance: to learn how to fall, get up, and laugh.

## CAMILLE

If we look at the life of the Impressionist Camille Pissarro, we can see the story of a hardship-induced fall, a fall brought about by the violence of others. It was during the Franco-Prussian war. Camille had been painting in the countryside around his farmhouse. Word came that the Prussians were sacking everything in their path and seizing farms as camps along the way. Day by day, the threat grew more real. Then Monet arrived with a roll of his canvases, asking Camille to hide them as he fled.

But Camille kept putting off his escape, until finally he was forced to flee with only the clothes he was wearing. The Prussians stormed his farmhouse and destroyed everything. They trampled his studio and wore his paintings as aprons as they slaughtered his sheep. When they had gone, Camille returned to an odd silence that covered the land. He saw a peasant woman kneeling on one of his paintings, wet and torn. She was scrubbing blood from her laundry with a stone.

All of his work was gone. Fifteen years of painting every day—gone. This was a terrible falling down, from which the sensitive painter never fully recovered. And yet, at forty-one, he began again, and all we have from this master was created from that day. The best survive because they only believe in beginnings.

## MARK

This illness-induced fall comes from my experience with cancer. I was barely awake the day after surgery when a burly nurse pulled back my covers. She wanted me to walk. I could hardly move. I ached everywhere. I felt as if, at the moment of anesthesia, I was pushed from a plane and that I woke after impact. I just looked at her. She swung my legs to the edge of the bed. I moaned. Then

she left and a gentler nurse appeared with a washcloth for my fore-
head. She looked at me with compassion, took my hand and said
in a firm whisper, "The rest of your life starts here."

I started to weep. The rib that was removed the day before was
now cooling in a jar in the lab while I, sore in every way, was
straining to get out of bed, and the door was as far and as close as
God. But she was right, and so, with much help, I put my feet to
the floor and began.

Learning to close distances was hard—two days forward, one
day back—but I confess, it was exhilarating to learn how to walk
with my whole being. Now I can say this falling down and getting
up humbled me forever. Within the year, I began to jog, wanting
to move till I felt like a tree opening to wind. I run now through
the streets eating light because I can.


## ITZHAK

This story involves a fall induced by something breaking. It wasn't
long after returning to life that I found myself at a concert in
which the legendary Itzhak Perlman was playing Beethoven's Violin Concerto, a very difficult though majestic piece that few violinists have been able to navigate.

My first surprise was to see the great violinist enter from stage
right with crutches as he dragged his brace-strapped legs. I didn't
know of his impairment. And having recently learned how to walk
again myself, I felt each drag to his chair as the climb of a mountain. Once seated, violin in place, he was weightless. Like a giant
turtle lumbering from shore into the sea, he was again in his
element.

Witnessing all this, so close to my own surgery, I somehow
received Itzhak's slow walk as a teaching and remembrance of why
we are here. All the falling down and getting up, it seems, is just

for this: for us to drag the parts that are left to the place where our gifts can fly.

Then, just as he was sweeping us along in the fever of Beethoven's dream for the violin, a string broke. He held perfectly still, eyes closed, and thousands of us held our breath. Time opened and he willed it not to move forward, not just yet. He reached in silence, his eyes still closed, for the nearest violin. The first chair offered his instrument and, in one sweeping gesture, this turtle of a spirit, who could barely walk on land, dove quickly back into the deep, bowing with a precise intensity the exact note in which his string had broken. And the concerto continued as if nothing had happened at all.

## TED

There is one more story I want to share. It centers on the miracle-induced fall of a young divinity student who was stricken with polio, and from somewhere deep within him came an unlikely voice calling him to, of all things, dance. So, with great difficulty, he quit divinity school and began to dance, and slowly and miraculously, he not only regained the use of his legs, but went on to become one of the fathers of modern dance. This is the story of Ted Shawn, and it is compelling to realize that studying God did not heal him. Embodying God did.

In small and great ways, we are each challenged to open the miracle of our lives by dancing where we are lame and by loving where we are wounded. It is an astonishing thing to ask of ourselves, and yet all our trials lead us there.

## TO THE REAL

It doesn't matter how our falling down is brought about, it almost always offers us an opportunity for transformation. It reminds me of an old Hindu invocation that prays for the unseeable master to lead us from the unreal to the real. We could say that falling down and getting up is one of the master's answers. It is one way that we are led from the unreal to the real, again and again.

Of course, we don't need to search for ways to fall. The harder practice is getting up. And these stories hold a secret about getting up: that however we may fall, there is this voice that speaks beneath our pain ever so quickly, and if we can hear it and believe it, it will show us a way to get up and re-enter life. This courage to hear and embody what we hear opens us to a more startling secret: that the best chance to be whole is to love whatever gets in the way, until it ceases to be an obstacle.

# How Can
# We Go There
# Together?

# HOW CAN WE GO
# THERE TOGETHER?

*Nothing matters now*
*but the instant where all I am*
*mounts like a wave for you.*

*The instant my hand parts*
*the air between us.*

If you should ask, I must confess that I spent the first half of my life trying to define who I am by what made me different from others. I kept asking God and the world to shout at me the ways in which I was unique and special. But somewhere along the way this all inverted. Now I spend my days trying to define who I am by what I have in common with other life. Now I listen for how and where we are all enlivened by the same timeless sources of energy and being. And while this confirms a common root system, it in no way means we are the same.

Similarly, I realize now that I spent much of my early life retreating from others in order to hear my own soul speak. While this was and is often necessary, it made me think that the deep, mysterious presence that makes everything holy was only available through my solitude. I now realize that the taste of true relationship hinges on our risk to know that holy presence in the company of others.

I had a sweet experience a few years back that forever opened me to this. It happened in Albany, New York, where I lived for many years. At the time, I had an apartment on the edge of Washington Park, a beautiful path-centered park seemingly designed to have people drift alone only to bump into other drifters.

It was the beginning of spring. It was a sunny day and I went to the park and sat on a bench. I was one of many coming out from under our rocks to warm and lengthen. He was two benches down, a gentle older man staring off into the place between things, beyond any simple past, staring into the beginning or the end, it was hard to say.

When he came up, our eyes met, and he knew I'd seen him journey there and back. There was no point in looking away, no point in pretending that we didn't know each other. And so he shuffled over and sat beside me. The sun moved behind the one cloud and he finally said in half a quiver, "How can we go there together?"

I searched my small mind for an answer. At this, he looked away and the sun came out and I realized: This is what the lonely sages of China were talking about, what the moon has whispered before turning full for centuries, what dancers leap for, what violinists dream after fevering their last note.

But I was awkward and unsure. He stared, as if to search my will, and after several minutes, he just patted my hand and left. I watched him darken and brighten in the sun, and vowed to look in the folds of every cry for a way through, and hoped someday to meet him there.

Ever since that day, I have understood his question as the heart of my own soul work and the work of our time: "How can we go there together?" For me, this old man brimming with eternity, patting my hand and walking on, helped me understand that this is the work of integration: to have our inner soul work meet our.

outer relational work. Indeed, how can we be who we are when no one is around and bring that holy presence everywhere?

His question made it clear to me that while it will always be necessary to travel in solitude to find the numinous center of what it means to be alive, we spend too much time keeping the truth of who we are in the closet. We spend too much time being *closet-authentics*, while the miracle of what is waits, ever so quietly, for our skins of truth to touch. Meeting this old man, watching him commune with God in the open, and having him shuffle to my side—it all made me understand what the Renaissance genius Pico meant when he said, "Friendship is the end of all philosophy."

For what good are all our questions and deepest thoughts if we can't be touched? This leads us to a core paradox: how no one can live your life for you and yet we need each other to be whole and complete. How often we cycle through this struggle: fighting off the influence of others to discover and be who we truly are, and then fighting off the loneliness of such truth in order to feel the sweetness of belonging.

This pertains to cultures as well as individuals. As America enters its adolescence as a nation, we can sense a need to mature with regard to this paradox. The further we journey and the older we get, the greater the demand to accept that we need others, socially and globally, to be whole and complete. In the nineteenth century, we were captivated as a nation with our *independence* and our manifest destiny to expand our borders to their continental limits. By the second half of the twentieth century, we were beginning to coexist with each other as we explored what Steven Covey termed our *interdependence*. In our own time, we are being forced to think beyond our own borders. We are being asked to consider what Thich Nhat Hanh has termed our *inter-being*. For this time, as both Thich Nhat Hanh and the Dalai Lama have said, the Buddha will come as a community, not an individual. So now, with the press of one world and the limits of any one way of seeing, we are being asked to re-imagine, "How can we go there together?"

As always, it is in the small moments that we begin. Consider the lesson of Native American children in Canada. René Lenoir tells us that when a prize is offered in school for the first student to answer a question in a group, all the students work out the answer together and shout it out at the same time. They couldn't bear for one to win, leaving the rest as losers. And the winner would be separated from his brothers and sisters; he or she would have won the prize but lost community.

Consider Contact-Improv, a new form of modern dance, pioneered in 1972 by Steve Paxton, in which dancers lean into each other, without any script, taking turns bearing each other's weight, taking turns responding to the flow of pressure between them, intuiting when to give and when to take, leaning on the other and bearing the other, rolling into and off of each other in a flow of balance. This is a wonderful analogy for the dance of relationship; for sensing the give and take that is always changing between us, as we take turns leaning on one another and bearing each other up.

Consider what Thomas Merton urges when he says:

The contemplative has nothing to tell you except to reassure you and say that if you dare to penetrate your own silence and dare to advance without fear into the solitude of your own heart, and risk the sharing of that solitude with the lonely other who seeks God through you and with you, then you will truly recover the light and capacity to understand what is beyond words and beyond explanation.

So, how might we go there together? Perhaps by risking the sharing of that solitude. Perhaps by taking turns in leaning on one another and bearing each other up. Perhaps by valuing community over achievement. In truth, each of us circles in the sky of time like the mythic *Chien* of China, an enormously colorful bird that has only one eye and one wing. Into this life we fall, needing to unite to fly.

# THE SPOKED WHEEL

---

*What we reach for may be different,*
*but what makes us reach is the same.*

Imagine that each of us is a spoke in an Infinite Wheel, and though each spoke is essential in keeping the Wheel whole, no two spokes are the same. Clearly, in a spoked wheel, the spokes separate as they each move out to support a different part of the rim. And clearly, they are all connected in a central hub that gives them the strength to form a wheel.

We could say that the rim of that Wheel is our sense of community, family, and relationship, and the common hub where all the spokes join is the one center where all souls meet. So, as I move out into the world, I live out my uniqueness, but when I dare to look into my core, I come upon the one common center where all lives begin. In that center we are one and the same.

In this way, we live out the paradox of being both unique and the same. For mysteriously and powerfully, when I look deep enough into you, I find me, and when you dare to hear my fear in the recess of your heart, you recognize it as your secret that you thought no one else knew. And that unexpected Wholeness that is more than each of us, but common to all—that moment of unity is the atom of God.

The spoked wheel serves, then, as an image for how we are

inextricably linked together. For without Spirit at the center or community as the rim, we find ourselves as unrelated and unsupported spokes drifting in time. We might cluster or gather around ideas or catastrophes, but we seldom discover our underlying relationship to each other and the world.

The heart of the paradox of the spoked wheel is that when we, as individual spokes, move inward and pursue the truth of who we are, we inevitably enter deeper realms of being where all souls meet, and there, we discover the hub of the Wheel—our common center of Spirit. When we pursue our outer work in the world, we inevitably experience our uniqueness as we enter more engaged realms of becoming, and there, we discover how our gifts form a rim.

Without valuing one over the other, Confucius beautifully described being and becoming as two ways that we are inclined to learn: through nature and culture. He suggests that when we arrive at understanding through being our true self, that is nature. When we arrive at our true self through understanding, that is culture. These dispositions to learning, like relational chromosomes, constantly inform each other and our way in the world.

Mysteriously, yet not surprisingly, the depth of that common center enables us to be uniquely who we are. Like wildflowers and trees whose roots begin in a common soil, the root of our individual souls finds its life in a common ground of being that waits beneath all individual selves. This is the shared sacred Selfhood that Hindus call Atman, Buddhists call Dharma, Christians call the Holy Spirit, and that Sufis call Qalb. The Spanish call it El Meollo: that which is deeper that connects the one to the many.

But what are the dynamics of the Wheel that affect us day to day? If we can accept our place on the Wheel, it is easier to hold and respect our unique differences. It is easier, then, to trust the mystery of the Wheel and to honor that no one way holds the key. All ways inform each other. Inevitably, all parts are necessary.

Without the rim, there is no wheel. Without the center, the spokes cannot support a rim. Without the spokes, the center and rim are useless to the living. This means that without community or relationship, we will go nowhere, except in isolation. Without Spirit and a common ground of being, there is not enough strength in who we are to support any kind of community. And without our beautifully unique selves, Spirit and community will never inform each other.

So where is your work right now? In your being or becoming? Near the center or the rim? Are you a natural learner or a cultural learner? It helps to realize that the closer we are to the common center, the more personal our work, and the more fundamental our efforts. And the more we move outward from the center, the more relational our work, and the more we are involved in efforts to manifest Spirit in the world. When near the center, we tend to share our learnings of inwardness. When near the rim, we tend to share our learnings of action and community and relationship. So where are your strengths? Where are you challenged? What do you need to attend these days to be both common and unique?

The image of the spoked wheel is not new. As far as we know, it was used by the third-century Desert Fathers, the early Christian Mystics. Like all metaphors and stories and myths, something essential, elusive, and useful is seeded in time, carried by one generation, left in the dust, and picked up by another generation— brought to life again.

It is interesting that we find echoes of the Wheel elsewhere. As mentioned earlier, Carl Jung defined the sacred, shared Self as both the center and the circumference at once. This implies a fundamental interdependence in being human: that we are more together than alone, and that we need each other to connect the center and the rim.

Even further back, Lao-tzu in Chapter 11 of the Tao tells us that:

> We join spokes together in a wheel,
> but it is the center hole
> that makes the wagon move.
>
> Thus, while the tangible has advantages,
> it is the intangible that makes it useful.

This speaks to the physics of the heart: how inner informs outer, how being manifests as becoming, how with Spirit at the center, our innate connectedness can shape and heal the world.

Never was this more clear to me than when I was sitting in a waiting room at Columbia Presbyterian Hospital in New York City, staring straight into this Hispanic woman's eyes, she into mine. Though we spoke different languages, we both knew the same unspeakable incline of this climb called life. In that moment I began to accept that we all see the same wonder, all feel the same agony, though we all sing and cry in a different voice. Though we couldn't say a word to each other, our meeting in the common center was instantly healing. I know now that each of us being born, inconceivable as it seems, is another Adam or Eve.

It's been seventeen years since that meeting, and now I accept my place on the Wheel. Through illness and grief and disappointment and unexpected turns in career—through the very breakdown and rearrangement of the things I have loved—I have come to realize that, as water smooths stone and enters sand, we become each other. How could I be so slow? What I've always thought set me apart binds me to others.

# ADMITTING WHO WE ARE

*It seems my sufferings have chipped
the coverings from my eyes
just in time.*

The Catholic tradition has long practiced the art of confession and, through the centuries, the true value of that art has been distorted, the way a holy chant loses its meaning the more it echoes. Carl Jung reminds us that the archetypal sense of confession has always addressed the inevitable need *to bring alive by giving voice to*. Yet to bring what alive? Among other things, the pain of our suffering, the tension of our doubt, the joy of our wonder; to bring alive the soul we each carry in the days that we have.

It's interesting that the word *confess* means "to admit," which itself has two simultaneous meanings: "to say what is so" and "to let in." For instance, "to admit the truth" means, at once, that we declare things as they are and that we let the truth in. It is the power of both meanings at once that helps us bring our soul alive. It is the power of both declaration and welcome that constitutes the true art of confession.

One important aspect of meaningful confession is our unending need *to admit who we are*: both in admitting or declaring one's self, with all our gifts and limitations, and in admitting or letting in who we are. For both aspects prove essential and one makes the other possible. It is a strange but liberating dynamic of being: When we admit who we are (when we declare and own our gifts and flaws alike), we then admit who we are (we let in the deeper source of our aliveness).

This seems to work like an inlet between the small pool of being we call the soul and the ocean of being we call Spirit. When we can admit who we are, in either sense, and give voice to what lives inside us, that very act opens us like an inlet and lets the depths of all being rush in. For admitting who we are lets the mysteries of life enter us. In a fundamental way, it is this exchange of waters between the small pool of our soul and the ocean of Spirit that keeps us alive. It is here that transformation begins.

Why? Well, one reason is that at the heart of admitting who we are is the spiritual fact that it is unnatural, even toxic, to withhold truth and being. Whales and dolphins cannot hold back the water that fills their blow holes, and birds cannot find each other or the light if they withhold their various songs. And we cannot stay well if we cannot *admit, bring alive, and give voice to.*

It is important to note that admitting who we are does not mean that we are required to always be vocal and yapping about what it's like to be us. We are touching here on a more crucial, if elusive, authenticity of being, where giving voice includes the shouting of a wildflower when it blossoms with no one around. It was, in fact, such a flower that helped me understand all this.

I was bumping around in the tender months after landing in my post-cancer life. I was humbled, grateful, tentative, in awe of sudden light and frightened by sudden sounds. It was a very warm day in April and I was walking through the remaining caps of snow in the woods near West Mountain in upstate New York. In the slight valleys, there were pools and pockets of mud. I was wandering about, dizzy with still being alive, unsure what there was to admit. It was then that I chanced into a wide clearing and the sun broke through, and in the center of the clearing, one small blue flower, opening before my eyes. No one was around. Everything else was still waking from winter. The wind swirled about the blossom and I stood before this small flower for the longest time. I watched until my projections of loneliness and fragility faded. I watched until I gave myself over to the slight blueness of a small flower blossoming in the open while the world was still struggling to wake. And there, I realized, not in my mind, but in my small pool of being, that this was a profound note of rest in the symphony of nature. This small blue flower was not waiting on anything or anyone. It was bringing itself alive by giving voice to its small blueness. It was admitting itself as an equal member of the mystery.

I stood there for the longest time, knowing in a flash that I, waking after cancer, was like this small flower in the clearing. How is it that I could be the smallest living thing in the woods and still survive? Somehow it involves admitting who we are. And as I venture now among the living, I confess to everything larger than me that my sufferings have chipped the coverings from my eyes just in time.

# THE SONG OF
# RELATIONSHIP

*To know someone deeply*
*is like hearing the moon through the ocean*
*or having a hawk lay bright leaves at your feet.*
*It seems impossible, even while it happens.*

There is much talk about relationship and all of it is warranted. As the great Jewish philosopher Martin Buber contends, it is the space between us that holds everything. This ever-changing *space between* is the ground of relationship, where barely visible threads are spun from what it means to be human. It is the web of relationship spun in the space between that holds us up. It is in this vital space between living things that the faces of God appear.

It really isn't all that complicated, if we look closely. The word itself, *relate*, shares an interesting twin root. Its Latin root means "to bear or endure," while its Indo-European root means "to lift or support." So, to relate means both. And isn't this the full terrain of relationship, to both lift and support each other, as well as to bear and endure each other?

If this is true, then we are well equipped for the job. The physician Tom Inui reminds us that human beings are *prehensile* creatures: beings born *to get our hands around*. He notes that one quarter of our brain is devoted to the use of the hand and another quarter is devoted to speech. The rest of our brain is devoted to *relatedness*.

Several traditions define the human endeavor as one of relationship. The Japanese ideogram for human, *ningen*, includes two characters—one for the animal we are (the creature that walks on two legs) and one for being-in-relationship. So, in the Japanese tradition, we, as humans, are understood as the two-legged animal that walks in relationship.

Yet nowhere is this walk in relationship believed to be easy. The ancient Egyptians regarded relationship as an art, even though what is created between us is often difficult to see. In looking at their hieroglyphs, relationship is depicted as the invisible painting that exists between people.

It makes deep sense. For isn't love the invisible painting that exists between us? This speaks directly to what my experience has been. Even now, as I bring to mind those I've traveled decades with, all of our stories, all of our laughter, all of our waking in the night to rescue each other—all of it is an epic mural that is nowhere to be pointed to, though I can see it as if it were all happening this instant. This is the power of true relationship: It keeps us close to the pulse of life.

The evidence of relationship is rich throughout the ages and can be seen in almost any aspect of life. Consider the genesis of wheat in Mesopotamia in roughly 4000 B.C. The humanitarian Lynne Twist tells us that, as different tribes began to meet and trade the single grains they grew, individual grains would spill and, quite naturally, the grains would mix and cross-pollinate. After enough trade, a mix of eight to twelve singular grains became the first form of wheat.

This early form of agriculture serves as a model of relationship; a model for what happens when we spill into each other and share what we grow. When true dialogue and relationship take place, a form of spiritual wheat starts to appear as a common food,

stronger than the individual grains of truth we know. It is this form
of spiritual wheat that relationship and community can offer us.
It's interesting that the root of the word *agriculture* means "generative field." And any time we lift up to bear each other and the
space between, we enter that generative field that centuries have
known as the art of relationship.

In her book, *The Soul of Money*, Lynne Twist also reminds us that
the notion of money was created in the 700s. Before this, we
exchanged goods and services. If you raised corn and I made
shoes, I would make shoes for your children and you would give
me corn for mine. We exchanged things more closely related to
who we are and what we do. In this initial system, which no one
designed, we directly exchanged a part of who we are. So, at first,
currency was an *extension* of relationship, but over time, it's become
a *replacement* for relationship.

Certainly, money has worked well, providing an unprecedented
ease of matching needs and goods. But over the centuries, as we've
grown more and more removed from what it is we have to offer,
the cost has been that we've lost the very human gift of exchange.

Indeed, it seems a law of relationship: When we stray from the
exchange of who we are, when we stray from the generative field
of relating, when we stop supporting and enduring each other, we
fall into the debilitating tensions of self-centeredness and the
pressing lack of Wholeness that self-centeredness produces.

A powerful way to understand this is through the medical lens.
As the physicist Paul Gailey suggests, health can be described as
the cooperation between cells and disease as the breakdown of
cooperation. A cancer cell, for example, ceases to relate with other
cells. For cancer cells replicate themselves at all costs: me, me, me
and more of me. Cancer cells feed by eating other cells. They are
the most ferocious example of a part living at the expense of the
whole. This touches me deeply, as my own experience with cancer
has helped me to see self-centeredness in a new way. Since my

journey through illness, I have come to understand that self-absorption and self-centeredness are a form of relational cancer: deadly to everyone. For just as cancer finally kills the life that is its home, so, too, does self-centeredness kill the world it lives in. This is why it is crucial to know whether we are living in cooperation with those around us, or just feeding off of the relationships that surround us. This is why it is imperative to understand the nature of our hungers. Are we longing to feel the health of cooperation? Or are we feeding off of others in an insatiable effort to replicate ourselves?

We are constantly faced with the chance and choice to cooperate or self-replicate, to deepen our exchange with others or to remove ourselves, to lean into the space between us and get our hearts and hands around what matters or to live at the expense of those we encounter. And regardless of how often we lose our way, we can always restore our sense of relationship, if we want to.

We have only to look to birds to learn how. I realized this when staying on Whidbey Island off of Puget Sound. One morning a sudden wind woke me very early, just before dawn. I couldn't sleep and so walked the timber-lined shore, and at the first trace of light, the birds began to sing, as if to proclaim the day and who they are. As it grew lighter, I could see birds everywhere, singing and flitting about each other. I know now that they do this to re-establish their place in the world. They do this to reposition themselves with regard to other living things. In a ritual of nature that is tantamount to divine radar, the light of each new day triggers birds to sing their unique song. And the multitude of songs bouncing back and forth re-maps the natural world every day. By voicing themselves, these delicate creatures understand who is where, and so, as day breaks the horizon, the map of relationship again becomes possible.

Each day birds everywhere re-sing who they are and their place in the world becomes more clear. This is the purpose of their song.

In truth, this is the fundamental purpose of all song. By this gentle miracle, we are reminded that the work of Spirit and the work of the world are very similar to this process. Only by singing who we are at the first trace of light can we refind and readjust our place in the world.

This brings us back to Martin Buber, who astutely claims that there can be no I-Thou relationship, no true exchange between self and other, until there is a self to relate to. And singing the song of who we are is one of the surest ways to refind our place. It is how we wake from pain, from sleep, from apathy and doubt. So, even when confused and somewhat in the dark, take the risk to voice your self and the map of the world will come into view. Sing who you are, even if you don't know, and your deeper instinct to relate will show you the way.

# THE LOSS OF ONE BRICK

*We must love one another*
*Or die.*

—W. H. AUDEN

Compassion has always been the key to whether we understand each other or not. And so goes the world. Like so many things, this is old medicine, carried in timeless pouches we call stories.

One such story goes like this. In the beginning, everyone spoke the same language. It was thousands of years ago in the land of Uruk, which is now somewhere in Iran. And the early human family, still of one tribe, devoted themselves to the building of a single tower that would be taller than any structure ever built. Their hope was to create a visible landmark, so that anyone losing their way could simply turn and look to the tower and find their way home.

The entire tribe was united behind this purpose. But it took much longer than anyone imagined. By the time the third generation assumed the task, the tower, still incomplete, was so high that it took a worker almost a year to carry the next brick to its place.

But the grandchildren of the original builders really didn't carry the same devotion for the job. It felt more like a chore for them,

having to build someone else's dream. Without their own devotion, it wasn't long before the press of the task consumed them.
Finally, one day, a worker carrying the next brick fell, and they
mourned the brick over the worker.

Of course, the broken landmark is the Tower of Babel, and it is
well known that, shortly after this brick-carrier died, the now-
heartless workers, pressed to finish someone else's dream, decided
to loot Heaven, upon which God *confounded* or *confused their tongues*.
They instantly lost the ability to understand each other. The
tower was never finished, and the human family, no longer able to
speak to one another, dispersed across the earth.

The medicine carried in this story tells us that the moment we
value the brick over the person, we lose the ability to understand
each other—we lose the privilege of a common language. And the
moment we agree to build a dream we don't believe in, for whatever reason, we become enslaved to the task.

We each carry this possibility in us daily. But there is an antidote as well, carried in another story. It seems that generations
later, a mysterious and powerful spirit came to earth, powerful in
his gentleness and his acceptance of human frailty. His ways were
somehow threatening to the conquerors of the time and he was
killed. But he had touched the lives of many in his short time on
earth.

One of his closest followers felt compelled to keep his master's
ways alive. But like the others, he was heartbroken with grief by
his master's death. Confused and torn apart, they wandered
among themselves for days. Then Peter was stunned to meet Jesus.
He had come back to life. What this did to Peter was inexplicable.

It wasn't long after this that Peter found himself before a crowd
of Jews assembled from all over the world. Between them, they
spoke more than a dozen languages. There were no translators.
But Peter could not be distracted by their differences. He could
only devote himself to the telling of the profound experiences that

had shaped and awakened him. Miraculously, as he spoke humbly and directly from his heart, everyone assembled understood him in their own language. They had, in fact, been touched by and returned to the one original language that all beings share.

The medicine carried in this story tells us that the moment we dare to speak humbly and directly from our heart, we understand each other. The moment we speak from the truth of compassion, we speak the same language always waiting underneath our differences. The mystery here is that when we speak from the divine center of things, from our own understanding of God, things become one again. So we carry this in us, too: the possibility of Oneness.

These are the deeper, perennial valuations: how to know when we begin to value the brick over the person, when we begin to get lost building someone else's dream, when we slip into speaking different tongues, and how to put the brick down, how to make the dream ours again, how to find the one tongue God has given us. These are the things we need help with, again and again.

The truth is that we carry both possibilities daily. In a moment of stress, in a moment of building a dream we don't believe in, in a moment of being more concerned with the task than the person doing it, we slip out of compassion. In that moment, we lose the ability to understand each other. In that repeatable moment, we lose access to our common, original language.

Yet in a moment of vulnerability, in a moment of suffering or acceptance, in a moment of letting the truth of things rise within us, in a moment of risking to be who we are in front of others, we can feel the life of others wash over us as we slip back into the sea of compassion. And in that repeatable moment, there is only one tongue.

In a modern world that ever presses us with deadlines and profits, the brick is disguised as a god, which, when we look to it, confuses our tongues, and we find ourselves alone. But no matter the language of my trade—whether it be the language of engines or organs or plants or computers or psychological states—when I am drawn to speak or listen with compassion, holding what is living above all that the living make, things become one. Suddenly I belong again to the one tribe that holds each other at day's end.

So, when we find ourselves speaking a language no one seems to understand, or, more important, when we can't seem to understand or feel anyone else, we need to ask, "What brick am I carrying, and has it become too important?" For the first step in regaining our ability to listen is to put that brick down. Then, magically, when we're not distracted by our differences, the one language will return. For the broken landmark we all recognize, no matter how lost, is not a tower, but an openness of heart that says, *Oh yes, we are of the same tribe. Finally, I am home.*

## A MODERN BABEL

Close to the one-year anniversary of September 11th, the *New York Times* magazine section published a very moving article, "The Height of Ambition," by James Glanz and Eric Lipton (September 8, 2002). It was an in-depth and very revealing history of the World Trade Center and how it was built. It was astonishing to see that the Twin Towers in their genesis are tantamount to a modern Tower of Babel, in which greed and pride and ego led the builders to value the brick over the worker.

Under the leadership of Guy Tozzoli, the New York Port Authority aspired to construct the tallest building ever built, an eighth wonder of the world, as well as 220 acres of office space. When the Detroit-based architect Minoru Yamasaki proposed a ninety-story structure, Tozzoli and his team insisted on a larger building, 110 stories, even though the safety of such a structure was in question.

Until then, skyscrapers were built using thick, steel girders that would crisscross the core of a building to give it structural strength. But the use of girders limits the amount of square feet that can be rented per floor, so Tozzoli insisted that another way be found. This piqued the ego of structural engineer Leslie Robertson, who was eager to devise a new building technology. He devised a system of thin steel spandrels embedded vertically in the exterior walls, freeing up the core of the building. This was done with insufficient stress tests in order to speed the construction along. Also, to insure the most space for rent per floor, the stairwells, which usually drape the perimeters of each floor, were stacked at the core of the building, and were walled with gypsum (Sheetrock) instead of brick.

When the attacks of September 11th happened, the bunched, Sheetrock stairwells burst into flame, trapping many people, and the thin spandrels melted, causing the towers to ultimately collapse. Had traditional girders and brick stairwells been used, the buildings may have stood longer and more people may have been able to escape.

While none of this would have prevented the acts of terrorism, this story reveals the greed and ego that made the Twin Towers ripe for disaster: the economic greed that prized rental space over safety, the relentless greed for greatness that insisted that these buildings be taller than any other, and the greed for innovation that led to designs and technologies implemented without adequate testing at the ultimate expense of human life.

So how do we live with these revelations? How do we understand them in terms of our awakening? How do we forgive and guard against such greeds? Though initially defensive, the engineer Robertson, when interviewed recently, said, "The responsibility for the design ultimately rested with me. Should I have made the project more stalwart? In retrospect, the only answer is . . . yes. Had it been more stalwart, surely one, two, fifty, one hundred, one thousand people might have gotten out. It's a big burden. I feel terrible remorse for those who died."

Like Oppenheimer witnessing the atom bomb destroying Hiroshima, Robertson joins those troubled minds who have unleashed forces they didn't quite understand, forces whose misuse or limitations they didn't foresee. It is true that creating new building technologies is not quite as dangerous as splitting the atom. Still, in replaying the archetypal lesson of Dr. Frankenstein, who trespassed where only God can create, Robertson and his melting spandrels, along with Nobel and his dynamite, and Oppenheimer and his A bomb—all painfully remind us that to be human is to *receive* divinity, not to *presuppose* it. We can come close and peer into the mystery, and even when blessed be touched by it. But we risk great violence and destruction, to ourselves and those around us, when we dare to rearrange the mystery.

That we in our time continue to relive these ancient struggles is less a cause for pessimism than a confirmation that each generation must take its turn in upholding humanity. In the end, how civilized and compassionate we really are depends on the lessons of Babel, as imperative today as then: how to know when we value the brick over the person, when we are lost building someone else's dream, when we fall away into speaking different tongues, and how to put the brick down, how to make the dream ours again, how to find the one tongue God has given us.

# THE FEATHER OF TRUTH

*It has all gone on forever*
*and it is humbling and freeing*
*on this rainy morning*
*to realize that my heart*
*which seems at times so vast*
*a pit of feeling that I fear I'll*
*never stand firmly on its rim,*
*to realize that this agitated*
*canyon in which I live*
*is just a pinhole*
*to the mysteries.*

## THE TRIAL OF THE HEART

Experience is a river that never stops coming. Often, to survive experience and unlock its meaning, we need to empty ourselves so as not to become burdened and clogged. This need to unclog ourselves is something all beings have faced, and each culture has initiated its own form of practice to keep the inner pipes clean. In human terms, this means keeping current, as Angeles Arrien says. It means we must keep emptying conclusions, judgments, and preconceptions in order to meet whatever comes our way freshly. If we don't empty and stay current, our heart can become thick and less vital, a narrow version of itself.

As a pioneer of transpersonal psychology, Frances Vaughan tells us that the early monastic vow of poverty was based on the need to empty, as a way to invoke a deeper form of listening. In its original intent, we find that poverty of mind reflects a quietude that can restore an inner emptiness, through which a Beginner's Mind can be re-initiated. So, poverty in an inner sense means a divestment of all the distractions that occupy the mind. It means an emptying of the *interior belongings* that keep us from the essential experience of being. This is very similar to the Buddhist understanding of meditation as a tool to quiet and empty the mind so it might touch upon the subtle essence of being that waits beneath all our human noise.

The Egyptians understood this need as well. In Gail Godwin's remarkable book *Heart*, which traces the myths and meanings of the heart throughout the ages, she describes the "Trial of Heart" ceremony that Egyptians believed every person faced at the end of their life. Once departed, each person's heart was weighed before the Court of the Dead. From hieroglyphics, we can see that the dead person's heart was balanced on a scale against an ostrich feather, which symbolized truth. It was clear that without an acceptable heart, no one could enter the company of the gods.

Everlasting peace for the Egyptians came from a balanced or open heart. Imagine, after a lifetime of experience, a person's heart was weighed against a simple feather of truth. If lighter *or* heavier than the feather, the deceased could not enter into the presence of all that is eternal.

If lighter than the feather of truth, it was believed that the heart had not experienced enough; had not participated fully enough in the journey to glimpse or understand the timeless truths. If heavier than the feather, it was believed that the heart had harbored too much of its experience; not surrendering enough, but churning too much with its backlog of envies and ledgers of wrongs and misfortune.

I find the wisdom of this ceremony extremely relevant. For the trial of a *living* heart is to keep experiencing and not to harbor all that experience. We are challenged to let life through in a balanced way in order *to stay alive.*

The Egyptian way models this for us. As Godwin tells us, "For the Egyptians, the heart was the seat of one's spirit and the center of the will." They considered the human heart the source of one's being and referred to it as *ka,* our double who lives inside our body. *Ka:* our companion, our guide, our inner counterpart who takes the best and worst of experience in and lets it out. And so it is for us. Without a heart equal to truth, we are lost.

As I explore my own trial of heart, I realize how much I struggle with this each day. I find myself trying to discern just how much I shy away from life and how much of my experience I am clinging to. It is an endless practice. And so I find myself involved in learning how to love it and not to fight it.

Long before I knew of this ritual, I experienced my *ka.* Saturated with chemo, I was injected with radioactive dye to see if the friendly poisons had weakened the muscle of my heart. There I lay, in the dark, watching my heart pump its blood. There, as ancient and present as anything could be: my double, moving old blood out, welcoming the new. With no words for what I felt, I rose from that table lighter, still unclear, but sensing that if I were to survive, I must carry less and watch less. Must put down the wounds that clog and weigh my heart. Must risk being touched so I can say that I am fully here. Must listen to my double who lives inside my body. Must listen to the red teacher inside my chest who keeps opening me to the truth that heaven is all around me.

## THE FEATHER NEVER LANDS

One quiet and powerful thing I've learned is that letting go is not just about putting things down. On a deeper plane, letting go is about letting your heart crumble, about letting yourself be rearranged by the journey of being alive. For the more we tense and harden ourselves, the more painful and bumpy our ride through existence. This is why grief expressed is freeing and grief held in only makes us want to join the dead. So often, in trying to protect ourselves, we hurt ourselves further.

To soften and crumble is not to die. It simply allows us to change. Too often, we equate change with death, when it is only a call to enter the unknown. Imagine it this way: *What we are* is a clear water of life, and *who we are* is the glass that holds that essence. Our personal identity is the glass we have shaped or been shaped into. But the water of *what we are* can fill and fit any glass, no matter its shape. It is very common to become so attached to the glass of our identity that we grow afraid, even terrified, that should our identity break—should things change—we would lose our essence. But as with water, spirit will fill any shape it is given or allowed to flow into. So our sense of identity—*who we are*—can change many times throughout a lifetime, and sometimes must, but the water of life we carry, our portion of Spirit, is indestructible and will fill completely whatever shape we assume in the world.

As a young man, I set out to be a poet. This was the glass that I poured my essence into. It was the identity that carried me through great seas of doubt. But the crucible of life broke that glass, and I deeply feared I had lost all of who I am. But it wasn't true, for the water of me filled a wider glass that I can only call my sense of being. The truth is that the same thing happened to me emotionally. I tried for so long to be the good Mark, only to have that glass crack, letting the water of my heart fill a deeper glass that I can only call the authentic Mark.

As I look back, there have been several, crucial breakings. Ideals have given way to the mud of real days, illusions have cracked to let the true sufferings soak the soul, and principles that proved too brittle have broken open to the blood and flow of life. Every abstract ambition, every plan for perfection and image of family that I chose to fix and harden so as to avoid the flux and change of life—they all gave way in time to deeper ground.

In truth, we are constantly asked to carry less, to watch less, to listen to our inner double, and to keep pouring our essence into the next glass we are born to. We never stop changing. We never stop taking in and letting go, and so, the feather of truth never seems to land. It just hovers in our truer moments with an airiness of being.

And after all this way, it happened yet again. This time on a beach while holding a book which carried the words of Buddha, a man who twenty-six hundred years ago urged his followers to rely on their personal experience, a man whose words have been spun into ten thousand threads.

I'd waited a long time and searched for a reliable translation, as if anything this far down could resemble his voice. And as I read in the sun, the soft breeze unraveled the tensions of my life, and I . . . fell asleep . . . and heard the lull of an ageless surf, and he himself came out of the ocean and we bobbed beyond the breakers, hardly saying a word, and he merely ushered me back into my life.

When I woke, I wasn't sure where I was but the sun through the clouds created patches of light and dark that were irresistible, and I began to wonder why birds sing at the first of light, why crickets cry at the hint of dark, why fish nibble at cracks in the deep. And so it is ours, to sing and cry and nibble our way free.

## BEING A FEATHER

Like some form of spiritual erosion, we start out wanting to hear the truth and falling in, we sometimes speak the truth and, if we suffer enough and are true enough, we become the truth. We start out wanting to know that love is possible and falling in, we chance our way as lovers and, if we suffer enough and are loving enough, we become the love. We start out wanting to hear the song and falling in,.we sometimes feel compelled to sing and, if we suffer enough and are loving enough and true enough, oh yes, we then become the song.

I hear versions of this in every story I am privileged to hear: from the young falling in, to the tired wanting to know, to the humbled compelled to sing. If blessed, we somehow become instruments for each other. One such story comes from a university-trained son who, when his mother died, went to visit his native father. He stayed with him for a week and, on the last day, they walked in silence far into the heart of the land.

There, he sat quietly as his father deepened his silence. Sometimes his father would look far off and the shape of his eyes would sag, and the son knew his father was carrying the things that burn where no one can speak.

It was then that the feather appeared. He tried to guess if it was hawk or crow or maybe heron, but his father said, "It doesn't matter from which flying thing it comes. What matters is that it carries us back and forth into the life above and the life below."

His father held the feather as if it were his own. "It carries us into sky life and ground life until both are home."

It was then that his father placed the feather in his hands. "Anything that connects above and below is such a feather. The quiet is such a feather. Pain is such a feather. Friendship is such a feather. The things that burn where no one can speak is such a feather. You are such a feather."

# THE RHYTHM OF
# KINDNESS

For thousands of years we have gathered in circle—
around fires, around bodies, around altars—
because we can't do this alone.

—WAYNE MULLER

Given the chance, as Mencius says, human beings will innately be kind, the way water allowed to run its course will always flow downhill. Given the chance, we will give of ourselves and grow by doing so. And given the chance, we will show how we need each other, even when we don't know how to ask. Consider these stories.

## DAY AFTER DAY

Not too long ago, there was a black coal miner's wife in Appalachia. She would walk in the morning and stand with her baby before her white neighbor's broken porch while their husbands were digging in the earth. She wouldn't say a word, just stand there rocking her infant and then shuffle over the broken path home. Within the week, her white neighbor began to feel pained by how thin and weary her black neighbor was. She invited her in a few times, but the broken black mother would never come in or say a word. She just stood there, tired and thin, with her little brown baby in her arms, looking longfully into her neighbor's kitchen. Finally, in some language below all language, the white woman realized that they were starving, and that she was asking her without saying a word to breast-feed her little baby because she didn't have the milk in her.

From that moment, they became an odd and holy family: the black and white mothers and the starving infant. And, day after day, the black mother would bring her baby down the broken path to the white mother's porch and wait outside while her newfound sister would rock the brown baby at her breast as their men wrestled coal from the earth. And, day after day, without a word, the black mother would carry her sleepy infant home. Neither told a soul. Again, she would come, and again they would hold the child together; in two brief moments, in the giving and the giving back. And the white mother would hush the brown child to sleep, singing, "Here's a bit a honey the bees ain't found." And that baby all grown has taught that lullaby to her grandchildren.

## THE COURAGE OF KINDNESS

In Germany, as the gray months of 1938 unfolded, twenty thousand Jewish children were given up by their parents, who sensed the Holocaust brewing like a storm they couldn't outrun. Secretly and with great sacrifice, they sent their children to England, where British families they didn't know took them in. This inspiring emergence of kindness is known as the *Kindertransport.*

Imagine the courage on all sides. Mothers and fathers sending their children away, telling them they would soon follow, but knowing deep down that they would probably never see them again. Imagine the wholeheartedness that opened so many British families, many struggling themselves, to say: *My God, we must take one of these broken birds in.* And imagine the children themselves—nine, ten, eleven—bumping along the European rail and crossing the English Channel, homeless, completely on their own, with no understanding of why. Imagine the ten-year-old whose parents in their fear charged her with getting them out of Germany. Imagine her little heart churning in the chill of England. Imagine the old gardener who took her in, giving her a flower every day, and saying, "There, there. It will all be over soon."

We can learn from each of their sufferings and each of their kindnesses. We can learn how to let go of what we love so that it might survive. Painfully, one father couldn't bear to send his little girl away, and pulled her from the train window at the last possible moment, only to have her join him in Auschwitz. We can also learn how to lift our heads from the daily hardships at hand to somehow make another place at the table for a new life that doesn't even speak our language. And we can learn from the children how to follow the scent of safety and how to go where life is possible.

In ancient times, God asked Abraham to kill his only son to prove his faith. In modern times, these mothers and fathers were asked to kill a piece of themselves so that their children could live. And what are we to learn from this? It makes me wonder, as we march in the glass parade, who should we praise? The one who needs the truth, though he can never tell it? Or the one who will not search, though he is always honest? Or the one afraid to lose, though his heart is big enough for two? After all the yellow turns of thirst, I cannot say. Only this. There is no limit to what we can give, thank God, the lesson at the end of youth, for as age ordains, there is no limit to what can be asked.

## BECOMING ONE WITH

This story comes from my own suffered trail and the words of a teacher more than three hundred years away. That teacher is Basho, the Japanese master of the 1600s. It seems that poets would walk great distances to his banana hut, where Basho would encourage a selfless sincerity:

> Go to the pine if you want to learn about the pine, or to the bamboo if you want to learn about the bamboo. And in doing so, you must let go of your preoccupation with yourself. Otherwise you impose yourself on the object and don't learn. Your poetry arises by itself when you and the object have become one, when you have plunged deep enough into the object to see something like a hidden light glimmering there. However well phrased your poetry may be, if your feeling isn't natural—if you and the object are separate—then your poetry isn't true but merely [accurate] and counterfeit.

We have only to substitute the word *truth* or *compassion* for *poetry* and Basho's encouragement becomes a living tool for us all. For the truth of compassion arises when you and the other have become one, when you have plunged deep enough into the other to see something like a hidden light glimmering there.

Now, there is no such thing as observation, only this *becoming one with* that makes visible all our connections to the world. From the Upanishads of ancient India to the Creator stories of the Ojibway people to the instructions of this Japanese master, we find the act of Oneness can be initiated by love.

Since my cancer experience—in which I was handled by both loving and misguided angels all stained with my suffering—I can't help but hear Basho's instruction another way. So I offer this version:

Go to the ill if you want to learn about suffering, and to their spirits if you want to learn about truth. And in doing so, you must let go of your preoccupation with yourself. Otherwise you impose yourself on the patient and don't learn. Your diagnosis arises by itself when you and the patient have become one, when you have plunged deep enough into the patient to see something like a hidden light glimmering there. However well phrased your diagnosis may be, if your feeling isn't natural—if you and the patient are separate—then your diagnosis isn't true but merely [accurate] and counterfeit.

I can't convey the ache that rises in me when reading Basho this way. For it was hours from brain surgery that I, in desperation, prayed for a miracle, not knowing how to ask. My head was shampooed and I was told to let nothing pass my lips. And I whispered in a scream to the Great Spirit, "Give me a safe, inexplicable way to drink again from the ordinary days and I shall speak of it when the winters are too cold for anyone to care." Somehow the face on my heart stretched in its pain, and I woke to the miracle of kindness, to this *becoming one with* that is available to all. Like a bird whose broken wing has healed, I sing this constant song: *Plunge deep enough into the other and a hidden light will glimmer there between us as we take turns being the wounded and the healer.*

## THE RHYTHM OF EACH

I know now that each comfort we manage—each holding in the night, each opening of a wound, each closing of a wound, each pulling of a splinter or razored word, each fever sponged, each dear thing given to someone in greater need—each comfort we manage passes on every kindness we've ever known. For the human sea is made of waves that mount and merge till the way a nurse rocks a child is the way that child all grown rocks the wounded. In turn, it's how the wounded, allowed to go on, rock strangers who in their pain don't seem so strange. Eventually, the rhythm of kindness is how we pray and suffer by turns, and if someone were to watch us from inside the lake of time, they wouldn't be able to tell if we are dying or being born.

The truth is that we need each other, even before we know each other, even before we know that we are in need. Like snow trickling down mountain cracks to form a stream, like streams washing over roots to form a river, like rivers meeting at the mouth of the sea, we run our course: destined to merge along the way. And it's the sweetwater, Love, that brings us together and that carries us on.

It reminds me of the lawyer in the movie *Philadelphia*, who, dying of AIDS, closes his eyes and swings his IV pole in his apartment as he listens to an opera. He swings about in the dark and softly translates the voice filling the room: "I am the God who comes down from the heavens to make a Heaven of this Earth. I am Love."

# THE EYES OF THE DEEP

The power of the human mind, alone, does not lead to full
consciousness. For the mind without the heart leads to a
failure of our depth perception, a failure to see below the
surface where the roots of our problems live.

—ROB LEHMAN

I began to discover that human maturity comes
as we begin to bring our heads and hearts together.

—JEAN VANIER

*In the beginning,*
*where I was touched by God,*
*before my tongue had word,*
*before my mind had thought,*
*there, in the fire I still carry,*
*the mind and heart are one.*

It takes us long enough to become thoughtful, let alone compassionate, and somehow, if we live long enough, without chasing our
tails, we start to discover that, helpful as it is to be both insightful
and sensitive, it's not enough. We are still asked to integrate our
mind and our heart, to twine the two, to know and see life from that

clear and deep perspective. But how do we get there? We know, all too painfully, that feeling without awareness is a form of misery, and awareness without feeling is a form of numbness. Both conditions plague us, no matter how wise or experienced we may be.

The epigraphs opening this piece name the seat of contemplation, that place below all duality and seeming opposites where our deepest eyes look onto the world. Often, it is this underlying sense that marks the difference between our brokenness and our wholeness. Often, it is this heart-felt awareness that stirs the energy of love to rise out of pain. Often, it takes a feeling mind and a thoughtful heart to enter the realms of paradox in which the deepest lessons of life await.

In our modern tongue, we have lost the word for this integrated place. In Japanese, there is just one word for heart and mind, *kokoro*. In fact, the Japanese ideogram for mindfulness depicts the heart and mind enfolded. It means "bringing heart and mind together in this moment." The Chinese, as well, have only one word for mind and heart, *shing*. Similarly, the Chinese ideogram for mindfulness means "heart-mind-now." Elsewhere in the world, the fishermen of Colombia created the word *sentipensante*, which means "feeling-thinking," as a way to describe the place that can speak truth. And Tibetan Buddhists have a phrase for the deep-seated knowing that such feeling-thinking opens. It's known as *klong chen snying thig*—"the Heart Essence of the Great Expanse, the Mind-Treasure revealed." Akin to this is the Sanskrit word that Eliot made famous in the West, *shantih*, which speaks as well to that place of deep-seated knowing. It means "deep peace that passeth all understanding." In all these traditions, the mind-heart is considered to be one perceptual organ.

If we look back far enough in our own tradition, we can see that the word *intellectual* originally referred to both heart and mind, but as we moved through the Industrial Age, its heart-meaning was cleaved. Somehow our preoccupation with everything mechanical divorced us from the Whole. And the integrated seat of contemplation that is honored in most cultures was somehow muted and lost in the Western world. As the rational mind became dominant, the workings of the heart ceased to be intuitive but were considered irrational, and empiricists and romantics were pitted against each other, until those sharp with reasoning are now called cynical and those replete with feeling are now called sentimental.

But the truth is that we still need each other. For only the mind-heart can open us to the mystery. So we are left with the task of reclaiming that integrated seat of contemplation. The Jungian analyst Helen Luke believes there is an art to such contemplation, which involves seeing with both detachment and involvement. She defines this awareness-with-feeling quite profoundly:

> [It is] an attitude of life, a way of relating to all phenomena, whether of the world outside or of the world within. To contemplate is to look at—*and at the same time* to reflect upon that which we see, with feeling as well as thought. There is no true contemplation without *both* detachment and involvement. For the most part people react partially to phenomena, to things, to others, to events, to themselves. Truly to look at and to see objectively, *and* to experience something in its wholeness, takes a very high level of awareness. All scientific observation demands long training and discipline, but this may be attained without involvement of the whole personality; not so contemplation, through which we may come to know fact and image, time and eternity, conscious and unconscious, in the smallest happenings of our lives. To put it another way: *When we begin to contemplate, we are seeking to discern that which Jung called the Self, at the center of our lives, in place of the ego.*

This bears unpacking. At the center of it is the belief that, hard as it may be to enact, we are not truly experiencing life unless we are both participating (involving our whole personality) *and* reflecting on our experience. Otherwise, we are only half there as the lack of either—not involving our whole personality or not reflecting on our experience—will keep us self-centered. And so we often end up compensating for our lack of participation or reflection by reframing people and events as props on our little stage to support our little theater of understanding.

The philosopher Reneé Weber makes this distinction, as well, in her fascinating book of interviews, *Dialogues with Scientists and Sages*. She says that the difference between a scientist and a mystic is that a mystic always admits to being a part of what he or she is observing. Of course, she acknowledges that great sages (scientific and otherwise) understand this, and her interviews show that sages, regardless of their field of training, have all arrived at a similar shore of perception, where the heart and mind enfold before the tongue begins to wag.

What this means in a daily way is that we show up with all of our care, and then let go of our attachments to what might come of our care. In other words, we can't know what is real unless we face what comes our way with our hearts in our mouths, risking everything. Something magical opens when we risk who we are. But, despite our dreams and expectations, the outcome of such an offering is frequently different from what we hope for. And so we are asked to detach and reflect on the truth of our actual experience, in order to understand the lessons we are being given.

We may not keep the person we love so dearly, but may become married to a truth that frees us from the tyranny of our ego. We may not land the job we so worked for, but may discover a deeper place of freedom instead. We may trip into the very losses we were so desperately avoiding, only to find, as Helen Luke says, "eternity . . . in the smallest happenings of our lives." Life is such a strange and relentless teacher who will not shout or repeat her lessons, but will pound us with repeated chances to learn them, if we remain too stubborn to hear.

For me, I kept chasing celebrity and, missing, would always fall back into something simple and beautiful to celebrate, never making the connection until almost too broken to get up.

When we can see with the eyes of the deep, one inner reward is an authentic and unimpeded clarity which doesn't remove us, but somehow brings us closer to the true nature of things. Edward Snow, in tracing Rilke's inner development as a poet, comments on this:

> He was amazed at his own increasing ability both to look unsparingly into his own self and to "look away from himself" and not to fear that he was constantly being watched by his own or someone else's observing eyes.

When blessed with such moments, we become humble conduits for the mystery of the Whole. This brings us back to the ending of Pablo Neruda's magnificent poem "The Poet's Obligation":

> So, through me, freedom and the sea
> will make their answer to the shuttered heart.

Often, in pain and fear, we *shutter down* one or both of our feeling and our thought—and so get stuck. This is what Neruda means in saying that poets are obliged to offer freedom and the sea to the shuttered heart; to the heart that has constricted its depth or clarity. There is no greater calling for a poet or lover than to offer others a way to return to wholeness.

So how can we see *both* deeply and clearly? And slipping, how can we restore our unshuttered sight? Like other oscillations of living—like opening and closing the eye, like inhaling and exhaling, like planting and lifting the foot when walking—we must become familiar and practiced in the dilation and constriction of the mind-heart organ. For the brute aspects of experience repeatedly disengage our heart from our mind and we slip, often unknowingly, into the oceanic turbulence of our feelings or the cold galaxy of our thought, drowning or freezing within ourselves.

It is another way that we need each other: to help us re-open the mind-heart widely. It is one of the gifts of love, to warm the inner lens open, again and again. Whether by ourselves or with the help of others, when we can let everything in, in any moment, things become luminous. Then all of existence somehow rises in that opened moment to restore us. When focusing completely on any one thing long enough, when concentrating our mind-heart aperture precisely, the majesty of life starts to reveal itself, again, in the smallest detail. These are the two ways in: through the depth of any one thing and through the clarity of everything immediate.

There is a Byzantine expression, "The mind descends into the heart," which implies that this deepening in how we encounter things is a form of spiritual gravity. Being such willful creatures, we often need to be stopped and jarred into letting things touch us. This is often the point of being broken. For when our habits of mind are shaken up, the mind can descend through the cracks into the heart.

I remember being so driven as a young man. I was an odd mix. My values were mystical and contemplative but my methods were type A and overachieving. I was driven and driving toward peace—biting my nails as I would meditate. But I was broken open and, miraculously, I awoke on the other side to find my center much lower; no longer in my head, but in my gut. It's as if my idea of life had melted like snow through the cracks of my life into the ground of me.

And everything changed. I didn't speak as quickly, and when I did, it was softer, always ending with a question. Through no wisdom on my part, I believe my mind had descended into my heart. I believe I awoke in the seat of contemplation, and from there the silhouettes of life burst into color.

We can only hope for this and welcome it. Through love and suffering and the practice of what they mean, the mind can be humbled to descend into the heart, and from that soft shore, the sea of deep-knowing awaits.

# THE KOAN OF LOVE

*Everywhere, what is inner*
*is bursting to become outer. Look.*
*The water swells and spits and sprays*
*and tries to leave itself constantly—*
*this is the source of waves, the*
*source of their beauty—*
*that they can't.*
*It's how we love.*

## OUR ATTEMPTS AT LOVE

I have known a great deal of love in my life. Whether I have suc-
ceeded or failed at love is hard to say, but I have loved as deeply as
I know how. Along the way, I have been hurt and have been hurt-
ful. I have felt vulnerable to the point of breaking and confused to
the point of saying yes when I meant no. And I have felt oppressed
and complete, by turns, both when in love and when alone. But I
swear by love the way a dolphin swears by the sea, and no matter
how I'm tossed and turned, I never stop breaking surface or plunging the depths. Ironically or justly, I am all that I am after fifty
years of such breaking and plunging, more completely human for
this flawed and turbulent wash of love, without which I could no
more have survived than a fish left breaded in the sand.

Still, I wonder about the koan of love, about the oceanic riddle of how to give of yourself without losing yourself. I wonder even now how to be compassionate and selfless without disappearing completely. How do we stay open and solid in the storm of human need? I wonder and marvel at all the inner evolutions that only being in love can initiate.

It was Rabbi Hillel in *The Talmud* who put these terse questions:

If I am not for myself, who will be?
If I am only for myself, what am I?
If not now, when?

Each speaks to the koan of love. Each if unraveled leads us into an apprenticeship of how to be in the world.

*If I am not for myself, who will be?* Why have a self? So that the Source like the sun can find you and cause you to bloom. Why a self? Because no one else can place you in the open but you. Why in the open? Because the wind is not visible but for the trees that stand before it, nor can love, the face of the Divine, be knowable unless a person stands firmly before the days with their arms out like branches and their questions fluttering like leaves in the open air. In truth, this standing before the days like a tree is what it means to be authentic, and without authentic presence, love is not knowable. This leads to the art of creating and maintaining a true and rooted self through which the wind of love can be felt, rooted in the open where the Source, like the sun, can find us.

*If I am only for myself, what am I?* To be only for yourself is to be a half-formed instrument that is never fully played. To be only for yourself is to be ready to receive, but never fully ready to give. The result is that life appears in silhouette. For just like music, love remains a silent, pretty idea if never given voice. So, it is the fate of the loving to be shaped by experience into a living instrument that is happy to be used. One name for this instrument is a true self, a self that both gives and receives freely. And so, if blessed over time, we carve and are carved by life of all that is not real, so we might know and feel our place in the larger symphony. If blessed, we establish our true selves.

This means that when we have been worn to the instrument of who we are, we are ready to be played. Then the events of the day—the dead bird stiffening in the parking lot, the happy child skipping in the mall, the soft neighbor reading across the street at night—then events like these make a music through our heart. And when we dare to live like a harp left in the wind, such unexpected beauty comes from being plucked by all the things that are not us. Mysteriously, when we can be who we are *and* stay open to more than just ourselves, the impulse of our gift and call becomes apparent. For the song that comes from life moving through us is how we know what's next. It's how we know which way to go. It's how we know what will feed our souls.

*If not now, when?* There is no preparation for giving of yourself without losing yourself, only the risk to try again—*now*. We can walk the shore and stall, but sooner or later, there is only the fear and thrill and completeness of plunging in.

And yet it doesn't matter how earnestly we try, this is still difficult. So much so that we can expect to fail. So much so that we might better rearrange our understanding of the experience—beyond success and failure. My friend and colleague Rob Lehman suggests that:

It is the notion and ideal of love, the impulse to love, that *brings* us together. But it is our failures and inabilities in living up to those ideals that *holds* us together; through which we can learn how to love and for which we can learn how to forgive each other.

So, perhaps it is our attempts at love—regardless of what happens—that continue to shape us more and more into what it means to be human. Perhaps each experience at love—both sweet and difficult—whittles us to be more humble and loving the next time around. Perhaps it is the wind of love—moving through our bare, essential selves—that makes such a tender music of our striving so hard not to be alone.

## THE HABIT OF OUR FACE

If our attempts at love shape us, then we must keep trying; despite how we flip from losing ourselves to hoarding ourselves; despite our confusions and compensations for not being loved or being loved poorly along the way; despite our loyalty to what our wounds make of us.

I want to consider the story of Narcissus here, a well-known warning against the dangers of self-centeredness. The Greek myth portrays a beautiful youth who falls in love with his own reflection in a pool of water. It is a punishment from the gods for being cruel to those who love him. There, he pines for his own image, trapped for eternity in his longing for himself. This is such a powerful archetype of what can happen to us if we are only for ourselves. Taken to its extreme, this imbalanced psychological condition of being self-centered can trap individuals in a life where everything and everyone is simply recast as a reflection of themselves. Not surprisingly, this condition is known as narcissism.

What happens to Narcissus, though, is not as well known, yet is worth exploring, as it bears on the koan of love all beings face. Eventually, Narcissus dies and is transformed into a small flower that bears his name. It is a widely cultivated blossom with thin, grasslike leaves and yellow or white petals marked by a cup or trumpet-shaped central crown. This is a curious reward for such self-possession, unless something else happened along the way.

So the question is: What finally happened that freed Narcissus from his own reflection? What enabled him to die unto himself and evolve into a flower shaped in utter openness to the sun? When and how was he worn enough, made tired enough, broken of his stubborn obsession with himself, so that he could surrender his image and become something delicate and beautiful? It is a secret we all need to know.

Did his will finally collapse, allowing him to see more than just himself? Did he finally see *through* his image to the depths under his reflection? Was this difficult, arrested state—being locked with his own image—some sort of apprenticeship of spirit that, if we're blessed, can lead us in humility to grow beyond ourselves? Or was his ego finally worn away as the self that carried it died?

Just what is the journey of Narcissus that we each must move through? What image of ourselves are we prisoner to? What difficult, arrested state are we wrestling with, pining after, disturbing each time we reach for it? What phase of self—born from the wounds of family or relationships—keeps us from knowing the world? What part of us must die so that we can be free? What sequence of inner evolution must we surrender to and endure to lose the habit of our face and to love like a flower? I'm not entirely sure. I just know deep down that love is what we are turned into and love is how we get there. And thankfully, love like flowers ignores all fences, and compassion like vines climbs anything that stands in the way.

## INNER EVOLUTIONS

Like those waves that constantly try to leave themselves, I have spent countless hours with the dearest of friends and strangers trading stories of the need to be free from the entanglements of others, only to long when alone for a home that will take me as I am.

The truth is that this is how we evolve inwardly: by separating and rejoining, each time rearranging who we are, each time re-imagining the line between self and other, each time feeling and living from a new bottom, a new sense of depth. This is how we love. This is how we grow.

For me, the greatest and most difficult learning of this culminated in my leaving a twenty-year marriage. After fifteen years together, Ann and I journeyed through cancer and saved each other's lives. We woke on the other side dizzied and fragile, unsure about the future, but certain that some mysterious grace had let us both live. I continued to live with a commitment to two simple principles: a devotion to the voice within and a loyalty to those I love. I never dreamt that these devotions would collide.

I said earlier that I have loved as deeply as I know how. What I never imagined was that that depth would change. But somehow it became clear that almost dying had excavated a new depth, a new bottom in my being. A new quarter of my heart was exposed to the world, and I was now called to love completely from that virgin depth. And the painful truth was that, while I had loved Ann as deeply as I knew how, in this new depth, I somehow didn't feel her there. Somehow, through no fault of hers or mine, we had become brother and sister and no longer lovers. I drifted in confusion and denial for almost two years. How could I leave the person who had saved my life? And yet, having survived, how could I not search to be touched in this newly exposed depth within me? And so, with great difficulty and pain for both of us, I finally ventured further into life; a small wave, lifted by the storm and rearranged back into the sea.

It amazes me and humbles me where staying true leads us. It does not keep us from hurting others. It does not keep us from knowing change and pain. But it does keep us close to the miracle of being, which gives us the strength of compassion to hold each other through the hurt and change and pain. I will never know the whole of it. I only know that the heart, like a wing, is of no use tucked, and distrust in the world, like an eye swollen shut, stops the work of love.

When looking back over a lifetime, I can see a pattern in how the soul like a wave becomes more and more a seamless part of the sea that is its home. It is a pattern of being awake, staying awake, and living awake. In my case, it is a story of how the life of poetry and the poetry of life have inevitably merged.

When I began writing books, they offered me an altered state of consciousness. They were a threshold to a deeper way of being and feeling. They offered me a safe place to practice truth. But after thirty years of being rearranged by life, my nonwriting time and my writing time are finally the same. All my becoming has turned into being. Now there is only just living.

I think the same can be said of almost any deep involvement, whether it be passion, drugs, adventure, work, meditation, or a love of nature. This is yet another aspect of the koan of love. Eventually, we move to, or at least are worn to, one seamless way of being and living in which all the heightened states we crave and experiment with are no longer heightened but of the same deep, long current we wake in daily. In this, we all aspire to an experience of life that lets the ordinary and extraordinary blend into each other, so that even our pain is somewhat numinous. Like the raft that Buddha burned once crossing the only river in his path, our challenge is to drop our special means of entry to the miracle-of-what-is and simply find the courage to live there.

There, as all the saints and sages attest, we stumble into an elemental love that exists beneath all motivation and expectation. There, we are bathed in love the way trees are bathed in light, the way shores crumble to be quenched by the sea. Struggle as we do, all choices, if true, liberate us into needing love like air.

# THE KINSHIP
# OF GRATITUDE

When everyone brings what they have,
everyone has enough.

—WAYNE MULLER

Recently, I had an old tooth go bad. It was abscessed and this pressured ache kept building from some elusive spot inside my head. It felt like my deepest moments of doubt. As I waited inside the specialist's office, I was growing more and more anxious. It's such a strange journey to be a spirit in a body. The Sufis compare it to an invisible bird carried for years within the body of a bird. But the longer I am alive, the harder it is to discern between the two, and the more grateful I am for both.

So there I was, fighting off memories of my cancer journey, trying to breathe through the pain, and falling into the fear that feeds on poor waiting. In an effort to distract myself, I paged through a book of nature photographs and came upon a full-page color still of a meadowlark. This delicate songbird had climbed the tallest stalk in a wildflower patch, its small talons gripping the stalk tightly in the midst of sudden wind. While its talons were clinging sideways, its body was leaning upright and its head was singing full to the sky.

I realized that the meadowlark holds on, in the smallest storm, in order to sing. Isn't this what we do—*hold on and sing?* Isn't this the art of suffering our way into joy? And if we *only* hold, don't we miss the point of our existence? This tiny bird was a teaching from God.

It was then that the doctor's assistant called my name. Feeling tiny myself, I closed the book, knowing that this was a piece of truth given just in time. For the next three hours they extracted the dying nerve from my mouth, and I held on like a meadowlark, my body slightly twisted as I tried to let my spirit sing. And from that in-between space, floating softly within my pain, I saw how kind this man was who was tending me. Though his eyes were intent on the thin canals inside my tooth, I saw behind his focus to his soft place. It was there that we'd known each other deeply, though we'd never met.

Suddenly, with a rubber gauze covering my mouth, I understood how cautious we are on the surface, and how kind and willing underneath. It is often when in need—when too sad to keep the mask in place, too tired to keep the wall propped up, too wounded to lift the sword—often it is then that we glimpse each other as we really are, stripped of all the things we think we need to protect ourselves. Ironically, once flushed out in the open, it is from the soft place that we guard and hide that kindness seeks kindness, and we are just thankful to be helped along.

It reminds me of a time when I was driving down U.S. 1 in California, just south of Monterey. I was aching and vulnerable, feeling far from home, when, through the harsh shore wind, maybe fifty yards out, I saw a large rock surrounded by a rough and churning sea. The rock was covered with all kinds of animals: willet, gull, cormorant, sea lion, seal, pelican, otter. All had found refuge from the hammering of the sea; each climbing, winging, hauling themselves on the rock; all living there together. They were lying on each other, exhausted in the sun. For each had been wrung out by the pounding of the wet hours. And each had found this rock-oasis, just out of reach of the sea, all of them too tired to fight once in the open.

It's clear now that this is how the wounded find their way, and since we are all wounded, this is how we find each other. Every survivor, regardless of what they survive, knows the hammering of the sea, and the rock we find refuge on is an exposed place where we finally accept each other; too tired from swimming to think any longer about territories; too tired to talk except through simple touch. And in that sweet, exhausted landing, no words are necessary. We can tell with the simplest of unguarded looks who has been jarred awake and who carries the gratitude that now opens the mystery of our kinship.

In truth, the wellness group I attended weekly when I had cancer was such a rock. The meeting rooms of recovery are such a rock. The thousand quiet rooms of therapy are such a rock. For those who have suffered into gratitude, tolerance is not a political position or even a principle. For those of us who have suffered, who have hauled ourselves into the sun, anything exhausted beside us is family. That we are still here, worn of our imagined differences, marks the resurrection of a deep and timeless gratitude that renews the truth of our common ground.

So the question that begs to be asked is: Can you climb the next moment, like a rock in the sun, to feel some momentary peace from the hammering of your days? Can you, in that mysterious yet ordinary moment, open your exhausted heart to see if you know the others who have hauled themselves there?

After enough tries, we might discover that a community exists beneath all identity and reason; a spiritual bedrock that waits below all casting of dream and netting of excuse; a kinship of gratitude that bonds us in our common experience of pain. For at the heart of every suffering, if we can find it, is God and each other.

This kinship of an opened heart can lead us to a universal perspective that can even reveal silence as a riot of love. Indeed, when we are humbled to surrender our claims of control and mastery, we are invited into a space where we are both completely ourselves and completely beyond ourselves. It is from this soft place of paradox that we can know the world from inside and outside at once, needing each other to withstand the tensions of that threshold. In this soft center, beneath our fantasies of commanding our own fate, beneath our guardedness, we are less victim and rescuer, and more needing each other to affirm and consecrate the enduring miracle that we are both ourselves and each other at once.

Somehow this makes me praise the spiritual fact that we are more together than alone. It is this sort of honest acceptance of each other that makes true relationship possible. It is a sense of togetherness that Hindu sages call *swanand sahayog sadhana*, "the unfolding of blissful collaboration." Blissful because, once opened by our suffering, we understand in our bones that hands are meant to join more than build.

It is here I must speak of a friend whose ex-husband recently died. Their love for their grown children made them find a way to stay connected. She told me that, as he approached death, Wendell knew where he was going. She said that late one night, he told his oldest daughter of a waking dream. He said, "I saw myself with one foot standing in the universe and one foot still on the earth." He said, "It was so beautiful, so peaceful. It was wonderful. I could see it all. . . . Why wouldn't anyone want to go there?" He said this with the deepest smile. It was from this place of one foot in the Universe and one foot on the earth that his love emanated. He knew that Source as God.

It seems the challenge for us all is to find and refind that sacred stance; to learn it from the dying, to bring it into our living. For such a seeing changes how we enter the days. One foot in the Universe and one foot on the earth; one eye in the heart of nature, one eye on the hearts of others; one ear listening to all the stories left like stars in the galaxy of time, one ear listening to the sufferings about to be told. It is from this place—that is within ourselves and beyond ourselves—that our love emanates. And it is gratitude that opens them to each other.

There is another famous vision of the earth that is relevant here. It comes from Emerson, who woke one day, recording this dream:

> I dreamed that I floated at will in the great Ether, and I saw this world floating also not far off, but diminished to the size of an apple. Then an angel took it in his hand and brought it to me and said, "This must thou eat." And I ate the world.

However it happens, whether dreaming when dying or dreaming when waking, we are called to bridge ourselves with all life, and to eat the world, not in a consuming way, but the way a worm eats of the earth till the soil within and without are the same. And so we are called not to watch, but to ingest and digest the world. In doing so, we cleanse ourselves and everything living. Isn't this the useful end of gratitude, to eat the world and turn it into love?

I was suddenly brought back when the surgeon, having sealed my wound, dabbed my lip. I heard him say, "You'll feel much better now." I started to well up, as if my tears—as if all tears—wait in hiding until it's clear that kindness is in the air.

As I walked back through the waiting room, I wanted to hug those fisted in their pain. But feeling shy, I put my coat on instead, and left the book of photographs open to the meadowlark.

# THE STRIPPING
# OF OUR WILL

Our will is only a gusting wind . . .

—RILKE

In his second book, *The Book of Hours*, published in 1905, Rilke, age thirty, offered a small poem without title:

> I live my life in growing orbits
> which move out over the things of the world.
> Perhaps I can never achieve the last,
> but that will be my attempt.
>
> I am circling around God, around the ancient tower,
> and I have been circling for a thousand years,
> and still I don't know if I'm a falcon, a storm,
> or an unfinished song.

His astonishing metaphor of "circling God . . . not knowing if [he is] a falcon, a storm, or an unfinished song" is extremely insightful about our movement from will to surrender in our time on earth. It's hard to imagine how a thirty-year-old might earn such deep knowing.

Rilke uses these images to describe the different levels of effort we invoke as human beings. He describes a physics of will here, and each image exemplifies a different aspect of will and surrender and the conditions that yield it. The images invite us to examine our own levels of spiritual presence.

To begin with, a falcon exerts its will to open its wings and ride the unseeable currents. It maintains its perspective and strength by riding the air. It survives by maneuvering the currents already in existence. Its will is one of alignment. A storm, however, is brought into being, shaped, and dispersed by the contradictory power of opposing currents. Its will is the result of a spiraling resistance. It has no say in how it appears, where it will go, or what damage it will do. This represents the reckless power that comes from unconscious resistance or being half-hearted. This is the will of the storm. Finally, an unfinished song relies completely on the voices of others to be brought to life. Rilke implies that all songs are unfinished and lifeless until sung. Once given air and voice and feeling, they manifest a harmony that is dormant between us; a harmony that seems only to result from a complete and humble surrender, both by the song and the singer.

A profound relationship is revealed: The more we surrender, the more we are touched by the life around us. Clearly, the falcon exerts the most will and is changed the least, while the unfinished song exerts the least will and is transformed the most. Yet the storm, strangely unpredictable and destructive, is somewhere in between. Brought into being by contradictory forces, the will of the storm seems to exert a violence that is not quite its own; it stirs up everything while transforming nothing.

The truth is that we assume these different forms of will at different times in our journey. But eventually, when blessed or driven by experience, we spiral through a stripping of our will into a mood of increasing surrender that always brings us closer to the essence of things. Yet being half-hearted (half-willful or half-surrendering) may be the worst state to be in—neither fully exerting ourselves nor fully giving over. It seems when stalled in the middle, we are a storm in the making, prone to do damage.

So, in your relationships, in your approach to life, in the way you circle God, what degree of will are you exerting? Are you a falcon, a storm, or an unfinished song? Are you gliding, disturbing, or about to be born? Are you exerting yourself to find an alignment with everything greater than you? Or are you a swirling disturbance creating havoc wherever you half-heartedly resist? Or have you found moments of total surrender in which you magically become the song that brings you and others alive? And just what is our healthiest relationship to will and surrender? How do we find it?

Not surprisingly, as a young man, I wanted to soar as high as possible. My ambitions, no matter how noble, were centered on gliding higher and longer than anyone else. But it was during my illness that I was brought through these phases rapidly and painfully. At first I tried to ride the currents of cancer, as if it were a wind I could negotiate. When that failed, I found myself in terror—trying desperately to resist, while fearfully feeling compelled to surrender—and so I became a storm, flailing at everyone near. And when that failed, I was reduced to an unfinished song, with nothing left but to turn myself over. Only then, ironically, was I able to find a quality of being that enabled me to enter some meaningful alignment with the greater whole. Paradoxically, it was my surrender of control and ultimate letting go—my acceptance of death—that opened a small doorway back to life.

The same questions can be asked of love. Are you a falcon with your lover, a storm, or an unfinished song? Do you glide, sight, and dive? Or do you tornado your way through? Or do you offer yourself as a song to be sung? It is an interesting exercise to look at our history of relationships in this way.

The strange truth is that, while we are being battered by existence outwardly, we are, in spite of ourselves, growing inwardly, the way that weather causes vegetables to grow. In actuality, we have little control over our time on earth, other than the degree to which we choose to root ourselves and stand tall before the wind and rain and sun. As human beings, this translates to being present and staying open. These are the efforts that cause us to ripen. These are the silences which, if entered, will sing. Though we can ride currents like a falcon, or stir up everything while transforming nothing like a storm, we are touched the deepest when we can turn ourselves over to life, like a song to be sung or something planted waiting to grow.

Like the silk that keeps the corn shiny in its husk, all our plans and strategies and delicate dreams have served their purpose once the heart pops up like a kernel. Now there is only to be sweet.

So dream as you will, plan to build your version of the pyramids, scheme to make and spend several fortunes. You can even hunt like a falcon for the things you want or love like a storm. None of it matters but the sweetness, the sweetness incubated in our dreams and sufferings, finally husked and brought to air.

# WAKING CLOSE
# TO THE BONE

*There are no rules now.*
*You who bore me, taught me, raised me,*
*Mother, Father, friends, lovers,*
*You are my brothers and sisters now.*

*All that you taught me to help me in life*
*Is no longer true, unless I find it so.*
*Your truths for you, mine for me.*

*But I, being some part child still,*
*Grieve for the missing parents to be no more;*
*Nor to be a parent myself.*
*No longer even a child of God but co-creator.*

*This is frightening.*
*This is glorious.*

—JANE BISHOP

I first met Jane in 1994 when Helen Luke brought me to the Apple Farm Community in Three Rivers, Michigan. She was a remarkable being with unusual spiritual clarity and peace, and I, among many, am more fully alive for knowing her. For Jane lived at the root level of things. Most of all, she listened to everything and everyone from that depth. Magically, I always felt that Jane understood whatever I was about to share. There was no need to translate with her. More than anything she might say, I think it was her complete attention that affirmed my small efforts to thin whatever I'd thickened around my heart and eyes.

It is as she declared: There are no rules. Given enough time and chances, we each discover the center of the earth, one at a time, and just seeing the center burn under everything changes the way we look at the stars, the way we hold the wood we gather. It changes what we see while making love. For me, this seeing from center has deepened the nature of how I feel. Now waves of feeling pulse and ache close to the bone. I used to think that ache was sadness, and so spent many years trying to get rid of it. But now it is deeper than not getting what I want or losing what I need. Now I feel this ache the way the earth feels its core grind about that central fire that no one sees. It is the slight burn of being here.

I am fifty-three, have been lifted and battered by love many times, have survived cancer and a cold mother, have tried to hold on to friends like food for twenty-five years, and all that has fallen away. I use solitude now like a lamp to illumine corners I have not yet seen. And, at times, I am scared that, after all this way, I will come up empty, like a man who thirsts for the water running through his fingers. But actually, I am only scared when thinking of the rules, which say I'm not enough. If we rip them up—no, Jane would simply set them aside—if we set them aside, there is nothing between us and the next moment about to happen.

Jane died last winter. I saw her three weeks before and she was calm and vital, her eyes alight. She loved horses and spoke of death as a pony with no saddle waiting in a meadow. She set things out to make her pony welcome. I loved Jane. I still do. And I marvel at how deeply practiced she became at living at this root level, so much so that curiosity and courage became the same thing. She taught me that listening and being kind are also the same thing.

It's meeting people like Jane, who speak in tongues that know the Source, that makes me believe there is a common heart beneath all human longing that burns like that fire at the center of the earth. And despite the weight of living, there is, within each of us, a luminescent heat from that fire that can be blocked but not contained.

At Jane's memorial, there were friends who knew her for fifty years and a woman she had met just once. Remarkably, they all spoke of the warmth and welcome of her silence. And over the piano there were two pictures of her just before her death. While we were singing, I kept staring at these traces of her. Then a horse whinnied across the road and stopped to outwait a cloud. I looked at Jane's gaunt face wearing out, more aglow from within, and it became clear. In the end, we are worn to the same bone, each of us hollowed to the one light we all take turns becoming. It's how that fire that no one sees keeps singing. For we each, in our turn, burn at the center under everything. It's how the song of a lifetime is played until we become the earth. It's how the breath of centuries keeps rising.

For so long, I didn't know, but now I confess: This rising forth of sheer life is what I live for. It keeps me alive. If I were a dancer, I'd use my gestures to scribe this endless rising against the sky, over and over, giving it away. Oh, the heart like a whale has no choice but to surface. Or we die. And having surfaced, we all must dive. Or we die. And more than books or flowers or thoughtful gifts that show I know you, the dearest thing I can give is to surface with the sheen of my spirit before you. And so I look for the truest friendships, watching the deep for spirits to surface all wet with soul.

# TELL ME YOU HAVE COME

Ideologies separate us.
Dreams and anguish bring us together.

—Eugene Ionesco

It is a great paradox of being that each of us is born complete and yet we need contact with life in order to be whole. Somehow we need each other to know that completeness, though we are never finished in that journey. Let me begin with a quiet and astonishing story.

I was at a conference in Florida, a Jewish-Catholic gathering in which believers of both faiths were trying to understand each other's suffering. At last there was a tiredness of debating ideas and varying points of faith. And so, weathered old souls gathered like birds appearing from trees to nibble at God's bread finally left out in the open.

It was late in the day, amid the scattering of coffee cups, that a tall, thin man with thick glasses and clumps of white hair shuffled to the microphone perched in the aisle. His back was slightly curved in a permanent bow. He started several times, clearing his throat, as if climbing the years to this ordinary day. He had been in Buchenwald and, in those early months of 1945, he knew the end of the war was near. A sudden air of liberation filled the yard with whispers. And one day, for some reason, he felt it was very close, the way birds know a storm is near by how the wind skirts the leaves. So he swallowed his heart and hid in a garbage can for seven days, enduring the dark and the hunger and the largeness of every noise without sight.

Then, after an unthinkable hiding, he felt the lid start to lift and didn't know if it was a German guard about to shoot him or an American soldier bringing him back to a life he could barely remember. In that instant, he almost collapsed from the pounding of his heart. It took a few seconds for his eyes to focus. Hovering in the metal can, he was still alive. It was then he saw the shape of the helmet. It was American and he began to weep.

There was a profound silence in the room as the old man wiped his eyes. As he started to shuffle back to his chair, another old man stood up, his voice shaking as he uttered, "I was that soldier," and they teetered to each other and fell into each other's arms.

I don't know how to describe what happened in that moment. In all outward appearance, it looked quite ordinary. Nothing around us stopped. Traffic came and went. The ocean surf kept breaking. Young boys kept stocking shelves in nearby supermarkets. But two broken pieces in the foundation of the Universe fit perfectly together and everyone in the room knew it. And more than these two were healed. We were all healed in a place that is hard to reach. It is strange yet constant that the breaking apart in the Universe is often loud while the coming together is often quiet, though no less profound.

Things will always break apart and come together. Yet, in our pain, we often lose sight of their transformative connection: that each cocoon must break so the next butterfly can be. And it is our curse and blessing to die and be born so many times. So many sheddings. So many wings. But in this is the chief work of love: to comfort each other each time we break, to midwife each other each time we're born, and to be the missing piece in what we need to learn, again and again.

My interest in this surfaced with a dream. I was walking across a very old and rickety bridge, one that had been repaired generation after generation, and as I neared the very middle, a young man, reverberating in his own inner turmoil, jumped into the fast-moving river below. I panicked and ran off the bridge and down to the bank where medics were on the scene, except instead of a physician, an Eastern sage, barefoot and bearded, was suddenly beside me. As they were dragging the young man's body to us—he was waterlogged and broken—I looked to the sage, who appeared unalarmed. He registered the concern on my face, took me by the arm, and said, "It happens all the time." I asked, "What was he after?" "Oh," shrugged the sage, "he was searching for *the fellow*. He thought he saw it calling him in the water. It happens all the time."

When I woke, I couldn't stop thinking about the search for the fellow. I immediately went to trace the word. *Fellow*, from the Old Norse meaning "partner, one who lays down wealth," which comes from the Middle English *welthe*, meaning originally "well-being." Fellow, one who lays down his well-being; not laying down in the sense of giving up or relinquishing one's true nature, but rather in the sense of unfolding or opening the way between living things. And so we are all searching—outwardly or inwardly—for the bridge of well-being, wherever we might find it. Why? Because in moments of being bridged we not only come alive, but, when in such accord with the Universe, we briefly become the Universe. So yes, I, too, am searching for the fellow—the other, the stranger, the conduit, living or not—who will serve as the bridge by which I might be joined to myself and thereby to the whole of God's Being.

This, then, is the purpose of the stranger: to enliven what is dormant within us. Once the deep thing is enlivened, it is our responsibility to keep what's dormant conscious. It seems that the strange messengers we come upon often serve as the extraordinary, completing agents we are looking for. Whether they appear as a lover or a crisis or the breakdown of a comfortable way of thinking, these catalysts often open us to a deeper way of living. Frequently, the underlying unity of things is waiting in the needs of others, if we can enter that completing space without losing ourselves.

So, though we bitch and moan at the demands of love, at how our plans are disrupted by real or imagined crises, it is the way we grow and learn. Though we resist it, and quietly curse how that special meal so lovingly prepared is getting cold because Uncle Harry, who has no one, just broke down on the Thruway; though we sigh so deeply when driving to get him, this is the curriculum that can't be found in school. It is a quiet and inexorable law that when I can't hold my head up, it always falls in the lap of one who has just opened; and when I finally free myself of burden, there is always someone's heavy head landing in my arms.

In truth, there is a timing larger than any of us, a readiness that comes and goes like the heat that makes our secret walls melt. How many times have I passed exactly what I need, only noticing the stream when troubled by thirst? The mystery is that whoever shows up when we dare to give has exactly what we need hidden in their trouble.

This was never more clear to me than when swirling in the turbulence of illness. It is from those who held on that I learned this. It is because of them that I am still here. I touched on this earlier, but it is worth returning to. Simply, I am well because others didn't watch my suffering, but entered it fully and then they felt love-sufferings of their own—which, at times, hurt them too much; which, in turn, forced me to nurture them—until, in bare, essential waves on certain days, we weren't sure who was ill and who was well. A solution that saved us all.

For once we cross over, once we leave half-heartedness behind, we can no longer tell who is giving and who is receiving. It is only the soft exchange of truth that keeps us alive, not just by speaking of it, but by entering it. There, truth and love are the same thing.

I learned this in an instant, two days after my rib surgery. You see. It was time. The tube had to come out. It had drained my lung of blood for days, through a slit in my side. The doctor was waiting and I looked to my friend Paul at the foot of my bed. Without a word, he knew. All the talk of life was now in the steps between us. He made his way past the curtain. Our arms locked and he crossed over, no longer watching. He was *part* of the trauma, and everything—the bedrail, the tube, my face, his face, the curve of blanket rubbing the tube, the doctor pulling the tube's length as I held on to Paul—everything pulsed. And since, I've learned, if you want to create anything—peace of mind, a child, a painting of running water, a simple tier of lilies—you must cross over and hold. You must sweep past the curtain, no matter how clear. You must drop all reservations like magazines in waiting rooms. You must swallow your heart, leap across and join.

All of this affirms a softer, more humble point of reference that accepts that when we give to others, we are, in vital ways, opening a mysterious process by which we are all equally transformed and healed. This inherent equality is beautifully expressed by an elder from the Achuar tribe of Ecuador, one of the oldest indigenous peoples of South America. When offered the help of benevolent Westerners, he said respectfully:

If you've come to help me, you're wasting your time. If you've come because your liberation is tied up with mine, then we can work together.

So, underneath all our notions of altruism, underneath all our efforts to maintain an identity as a giving person, underneath all the frustrations that arise from the inevitable inconvenience of true giving—there waits the journey of our liberation in which we need each other in unimagined ways to survive all the breaking apart and coming together that life demands. And not surprisingly, the doorway to that journey is often the awakening of our compassion.

Amazingly, despite our pain and loneliness, despite our fear of getting too involved, we are connected in a timeless place of safety that is always just below the surface. And each time we are needed, we are invited to break through that isolating surface. If we can respond in those moments from the heart of our true nature, we can stumble into that place of true meeting where our liberation is the work and our honest friendship is the tool.

In truth, when we treat what we encounter as thoroughly alive, we tend to put things together. And putting things together somehow brings us below the surface, into a living friendship with the Universe. It is interesting to note that the German root of the word *friendship, berg-frij,* means "place of high safety." This joining below the doorway of need drops us into that mysterious place of high safety.

Whether we break through or are broken through, we land in the place where we are each other. Let me share another story. My dear friend's mother is close to death. A few months back, they found her unconscious on the floor of her apartment. She had an infection in her liver. It set her on fire with a fever of a hundred and five. In the ambulance, they packed her in ice. All the while, in her delirium, she had this waking dream. She was drifting through a crowd of people from all over the world, everyone wearing a particular kind of face—anger, sadness, fear, laughter, annoyance, pain—and suddenly, at once, everyone began to remove their faces as if they were masks. And underneath, every single life had the face of Jesus.

Once back in her body and awake, she was hesitant to speak of this. It seemed, she said, not for human ears. Of course, it is something profound that we sorely need to hear. For under the many masks of our human experience, we all share the same face of God. Yes, under the thousand faces of pain, we share the same faceless heart. So tell me you have come, so we might help each other fall through our need to the center where we are joined.

# Honoring
# the
# Mystery

# HONORING THE MYSTERY

*It seems so far away*
*but is next to us all the time.*

*So, be my friend, my teacher*
*and show me when I forget.*

The mystery is everywhere yet somewhat unknowable, like the ocean a fish can't fully see because it lives inside it. Just this way, the sea of mystery we live in holds us all, moves through us clearly, and keeps us alive. It does this with or without our consciousness and with or without our help. But honoring the mystery is what opens us to the powers of wholeness.

And this unknowable totality that we live in is larger than any either-or, deeper than any right or wrong, more embracing than any attempt to separate our joy from our suffering, and more possible than any one notion of good or bad. We can describe this totality as the ground of being underneath all life, in which all things are rooted. And there are many things, uplifting and painful, that can open us to this totality. Paradox, ambiguity, uncertainty, the tension of opposites, pain, joy, love, wonder, curiosity, sorrow, gratitude, song—all of these and more can jar us below our maps of life into the unending unity of things.

So, to honor the mystery is not just to glimpse the Whole or even to acknowledge the Whole, but to live our days with that Wholeness at the center of our understanding. Charles Fillmore, the founder of the Unity Church, sees this as the value of bearing witness to the mystery:

> The purpose of *affirmation* is to establish in consciousness a broad understanding of the divine principles on which all life and existence depend.

We could even say that to affirm the mystery is to lean into the various moments that drive us or compel us beneath our surface notions of life. In this way, honoring the mystery means staying open to the many things that invite us or force us to widen and deepen our sense of unity and reality.

When I was younger, I think I misused my feelings. I would try to ride the pleasant ones and endure the difficult ones. But I never really followed them, as teachers, to the reality that held them all, let alone embrace that unified reality. Then I had a dream in which I was afraid to enter a sweat lodge when a Native Elder entered before me, saying, "You must sweat through your holy feelings. They are the gateway." Over time, this has led me to believe that the mystery of Wholeness is not just an idea, but a deeper reality that is always near. In watching life, we can draw its silhouette and speak to its geography, but only by *living* life do *we* become three-dimensional. This seems so obvious. Yet we often hover and never enter that deeper sense of things, afraid we won't make it through the initial wave of feeling that is its threshold. The spirit in us, however, is strong enough to move through the openings that feeling provides. It is like breaking trail into an open field. Whether we praise, listen, hold or suffer, or wait and withstand, when we follow the path of feeling all the way to its source, we slip through into the meadow.

Even understanding this, to honor the unity of things evokes a devotion of seeing whereby we keep trying to view the parts of life *through the lens of the Whole and from the embrace of center,* which is different from adding parts together to form a whole or following the parts to discover the whole. Consider the difference between cells and a person. Cells alone are unable to do anything, but when empowered together by the mystery of life, here we are: waking, standing, reaching, all with this remarkable consciousness to listen to each other, to sit and cross our legs, or to walk out into the day.

Yet even when we glimpse the mystery through our wonder or our pain, we often reflex back into a partial walk through life. In addition to this, affirming and maintaining our sense of unity is even more difficult in a culture that is always breaking things down. But ultimately, it is as the Taoist philosopher Chuang Tzu says:

> Great knowledge sees all in one.
> Small knowledge breaks down into the many.

The power of this understanding as a way to build our days cannot be overstated. For it makes a difference if we view the waters of the earth as seven separate oceans or one magnificent sea. It makes a difference if we view the lands of the earth as separate nations or one massive home. It makes a difference if we view those living on earth as separate peoples or one family of humankind. A liberating difference if we delineate between humans and animals and plants and stones or if we affirm the common thread of life in all things.

And while we are, of course, uniquely ourselves, we can affirm, despite our separate streams of thinking, that we are of one universal, oceanic mind. We can affirm, despite our separate veins of feeling, that we are of one universal heart. And when we love, though we love different people in different ways across a lifetime, we can affirm that they are all part of the same, nameless love.

Thus, if we can open ourselves to the mystery of it all, if we can glimpse the Whole, affirm the Whole, commit to leaning into life until it drops us beneath our surface maps of reality, we may discover that, though we pray to the many faces of God, each is a changing wave in a sea of divine being in which we are tiny fish. And anything in our experience that causes us to trip below our preferences and smaller ways of seeing—any circumstance that awakens us to that divine sea—is a holy gift.

Earlier, we spoke about sinking through our moments of suffering or emptiness into a feeling of isolation and despair. So, it might seem confusing to talk here about falling through or dropping below our surface understanding of things. Of course, these things are related. Just like the kinship between passion and desire, the difference here is thin. When we speak about sinking into despair, it refers to a turning into oneself that removes us from our connection to all other aspects of life, and so we sink into a dark and seemingly unforgiving place. When we talk here about falling through, this refers to a necessary deepening that brings us beneath our smaller ways of thinking and our personal forms of illusion into a bedrock of existence that holds all of our differences.

So, let me offer a personal example of when I've fallen through my maps of relationship into the one stream of love. It involves my former wife, Ann. When we began, we were eager to be loved. Everything held wonder in a secret place that to us was shouting like a waterfall. I can't tell the whole story here except to say that thirty years have passed and we have been friends, lovers, have saved each other's lives, been ex-lovers, difficult friends, have felt discounted and betrayed, have almost walked away, have landed in the sea of forgiveness, and have somehow found love in other eyes. And blessedly, we have been worn beneath all these roles by love and suffering into a place of connection where the threads of life join. Blessedly, we don't know what to call each other now.

Today we live states away and she is losing her sight and I am creaky in the knees, and still the same wind moves through our hearts. Somehow we have been dropped into the mystery, below role, dropped into the unity where it is enough to say, simply—it has something to do with love.

Always, when blessed enough to be worn of our stubbornness, we are humbly awakened to our deep connection to others. And just last week, in a small place, I was listening to a folksinger with Susan, when a part of his song opened something and I realized I have never been happier, have never been more in love, never closer to the fragile pulse of things. But the opening didn't stop there. It drew me in until, like leaning over the edge of a cliff, the feeling took me down to the beginning and I realized that loving Ann and others is where it began. And I just wanted to say thank you, and to confess how strange and perfect that the ground we learn to dance on is an old love's heart. I pray that loving me has led them somewhere, too. Yet somehow I think that they have stared briefly at the moon in such a moment, feeling the underlying depth, like me. Funny, how we start out all arms and legs and wild ideas, and the years round us down till we are nothing but limbless hearts.

It comes and goes, this sense of mystery that surrounds us. Just now, this morning, over coffee, it is raining, gently. And the birds are beginning to sing, while Susan is sleeping, our dog curled in my space. For some reason, I've fallen again into the quiet basin of my heart where all loves mix. And there, the friends and lovers and strangers and the family I no longer talk to—there, they have all softened like cardboard drifting in the ocean.

The light rain at the window is saying, *Don't. Don't think too hard— just swim.* Can it be—that all our lives we're just oddly shaped cups and mugs: sometimes clear, sometimes not, sometimes chipped, sometimes too hot to hold? Can it be—the whole sorry struggle for a self is just to have something sturdy enough to carry the love?

All I can say is that it can be painful or sweet, but this is the nature of transformation: Some moment or circumstance becomes an unexpected doorway to the mystery. We never know how it will appear or how we will be drawn into it. It could be through the sinking feeling that comes from a letter never answered, the one in which you declared your love in such a desperate way, admitting to everything. Or when the shell you brought all the way from the Philippines is dropped by some loud stranger you never wanted to show it to in the first place. It could all unravel the moment the shell shatters on your hardwood floor.

Or quite simply on a summer bench, your eyes closed, when the sun seems to vanish, the heat gone, though bees begin to fly, and in that moment, you're suddenly not sure where all this hard work has taken you. It could happen anywhere that you linger too long, anywhere you stop hauling and counting, anywhere your mind spills its tangle of agendas.

Often, it comes with the relaxation of great pain. When the hip finally mends enough to step, that step opens the world. Or it could be waiting in the moment your strength of ambition is broken by seeing a bird run over in a soundless turn. Or when watching trees slip into winter before you're ready. And though I can't explain its comings and goings, I just know that when I feel I could crumble, and all my pain feels like salt waiting for a wave, I am close. We are close. When the elements in all their fury reshape our weary eyes, it is God's kiss: gentle as erosion, outlasting the ten thousand schemes.

At the heart of it, this being opened unexpectedly into the unity of things is a nameless ritual. And how we respond to these openings determines whether we feel a part of something or a part of nothing. We are often prompted by an uneasiness. You can, for example, feel that something is missing. And you can try to forget that you are empty, by reading hundred-year-old novels of love or by planting dozens of bulbs for a spring yet to come. Or you can try to fix what you see as broken in others until they call you kind. Or you can look into the hidden gears of the world until others think you intelligent. And when nothing reaches you, you can run into things until old ways crack. And when exhausted, you might feel some spot of peace that's been waiting beneath your name. Then you can secretly feel the pain of wanting to be touched by everything. And not being touched, you might feel lost, and being touched, you can suddenly feel that there might be such a thing as joy. Then something might make you climb higher than all obstacle. And smelling the fumes of your birth, you might risk that all thoughts are clouds and burn them away with the heat of your being.

And yet you may be asked to wait, sensing the unity just out of view. So what to do? How to proceed? This leads me to three teachers who, each in their own way, offer some guidance. First, Cezanne, who said, "I leave spaces because I'm not certain." For if there are no spaces, there is nowhere to drop through into the unity that holds us. Second, Gandhi, when he said, "If you don't tell your story, you betray it." For telling our story is the surest way to pry the world and its maps open. And third, Robert Frost, who mused, "We dance around in a circle and suppose, while the secret sits in the middle and knows." For only by leaving spaces and telling our story, over and again, can we find each other in the circle we are born into.

In truth, it seems that to honor the mystery, we are called to live from the center, trying to bring our inner lives and outer lives together *as a starting point* from which to enter the days. For we access a different sense of wholeness when integrated than divided.

When exhausted from the seeming complexity of life and the demands of others, it makes a difference to know that when you cup water to your tired face, it is from the one magnificent and nameless sea. And when you feel the pain of love—mis-given or mis-received—break your heart, it helps to know that what breaks open is the covering to your soul. It helps to know that what is opened by the break is the place where mystery lets flow a portion of all the love there ever was.

# THINGS AS THEY ARE

There's a thread you follow. It goes among
things that change. But it doesn't change.
People wonder about what you are pursuing.
You have to explain about the thread.
But it is hard for others to see.
While you hold it you can't get lost.
Tragedies happen; people get hurt
or die; and you suffer and get old.
Nothing you do can stop time's unfolding.
You don't ever let go of the thread.

—WILLIAM STAFFORD

## THE THREAD

We could spend a great deal of time guessing what the thread is. In many ways, this whole book has been trying to name the thread and the many ways to see it, to hold it, and to share it with others. But the truth is that, like so many things that matter, we each have to find it and make use of it ourselves. Still, it is worthwhile to discuss these things.

When we talk about a thread that *goes among things that change, though it doesn't change*, we are returning to a notion of integrity whereby we keep meeting the outer world with our inner world.

And, as we have seen, it is often difficult to keep this powerful aspect of truth in view. Still, waiting underneath all our hopes and sufferings, there is this thread of truth that lives in the ground of reality. It is known as *Things As They Are.*

Now, we need to say a few things about this. For, certainly, things as they are evokes a different truth for me, as I write this, than for the four-year-old girl in a soldier's arms, as he sits in the dust of Rifa in northern Iraq minutes after her mother was killed. And this, in turn, is different yet from the soldier's sense of things as they are, as he rocks this sudden orphan.

Clearly, we are talking about a bedrock sense of is-ness that holds the spectrum of human experience—at once true to each situation *and* true to the larger truth that holds them all. It is this common, indestructible is-ness that is our home, regardless of the crises we land in or the losses we suffer. It is why hearing each other's stories, no matter how different, can lead us to a mysterious strength that lines the underside of all story.

So often, our pain understandably blinds us to the balance of things as they are, which includes everything at the time not in pain. And too often, our joy, less understandably, blinds us to that same balance, which includes everything at that time not in joy.

The truth is that we do not have to quarantine our experience for it to be legitimate. We do not have to minimize the suffering or joy of others to validate our own. For whether we are in pain or in a moment of joy, our particular experience is not diminished by welcoming things as they are. Rather, what we are feeling is set in a unified context of other life living around us, a context that is ultimately empathetic and humbling, and therefore empowering. In reality, to embrace things as they are opens us to the power of compassion.

Inevitably, when we are clear, someone is confused. When we are consumed with fear, someone is knowing safety. When we are empty, someone is exceedingly full. Unfortunately, we quickly forfeit the strength of this totality when we *compare* our reality to others'. For the power of things as they are waits in our willingness to allow these different realities to touch and affect each other. Even within our own lives, we tend to compare a happy time with a sad time, a time of ease with a time of struggle, and so, lose the overall richness of an evolving life that has an is-ness of its own.

Again, for me, my illness has been a teacher. For I have outlived a tumor pressing on my brain, have had my eighth rib removed, and though I wept in the tub at the gash in my side, at the fact that I could be slit open so easily like a bull pumped up for market, that cut some-how opened me to more lives than just my own. Now I understand in a palpable way that my experience, though it contributes, is not the leading description of the world or of life on earth. And the gift of knowing things as they are, even briefly, is that I now understand that to be broken is no reason to see all things as broken.

Strangely, knowing when I am hurting that the whole world isn't hurting no longer makes me sad and lonely. And knowing when I am joyous that the whole world isn't joyous no longer muffles me with guilt. Rather, these poignant moments are touching and com-pleting in the sense that life is incredibly various and buoyant beyond our imagination or control. There is a mystical strength in the totality of our human experience. And holding on to this know-ing is, in itself, a guide through the chaos. As William Stafford so wisely puts it, *while you hold on to the thread, you can't get lost.* But being human, we do get lost. So what is the nature of things as they are, and how do we return to it when we've lost its power?

## NOT TURNING ONE THING INTO ANOTHER

In his book *Sabbath: Restoring the Sacred Rhythm of Rest,* my dear friend Wayne Muller reminds us that, in the Jewish tradition, there are thirty-nine guidelines for entering and holding the Sabbath. And all have to do with *not turning one thing into another.* For instance, not turning stones into a wall or wood into beams. This fundamental request is at the heart of all rest: *to leave things as they are.* The assumption here holds the paradox that while we can build and create and better our condition, things are inherently fine as they are. It is a notion of life we can easily lose sight of.

But when we stop turning one thing into another, when we slow down and rest, we are privileged to enter the bare, essential realm of things as they are. In this, rest and truth are forever linked. One gives rise to the other. Both offer us the world underneath all agitation and illusion.

It is helpful to apply this ancient instruction to our daily patterns of thought and feeling. For when we stray from peace and from the truth of things as they are, it is often because we have been busy turning one thing into another in our minds and hearts. So when tired and confused, slow down and rest. When you lose your grasp of the Whole, be quiet and stop turning. When you are drowning in your own pain, stop stirring up the water so you can see the bottom. Stop turning pain into fear. Stop turning the unknown into a practice ground for worry. Stop turning gestures of doubt or love into measurements of your worth. While we are blessed with consciousness, we often work it like ants, furiously moving things around in our minds, constantly turning one thing into another; never resting, never giving ourselves the chance to settle into the raw beauty of things as they are.

Too many times, our discomfort with not-knowing prompts us to prematurely turn one thing into another before it can present itself more completely. A very simple, if painful, example is when, having offered our heart, we can't bear the wait for that treasured response. And so we turn the silence into our worst fear or best hope, never giving things as they are the time to show its truth. During the medical gauntlet, this was a constant challenge, for no one, including the doctors, knew where my life was leading. Yet everyone, in their discomfort with not-knowing, offered scenario after scenario of ways that I would die. And my job was somehow not to turn the waiting into something else that would have me already dead.

I think that's the key. Life takes time to live. It takes time to unfold its more lasting truths. And our job is somehow not to turn the waiting into something else that has us already dying. This is the wisdom of the Sabbath, carried within us in the quiet center of every moment. It is there in the quiet, tiny space between the beats of our heart. There, we can always relearn how to not turn one thing into another. And the truth we know—the peace we weave from one centered moment to the next—is the thread.


## NEITHER DENY NOR INDULGE

Still, it is often just as hard to not turn one thing into another as it is to return to things as they are. And we might rightly ask again: How do we keep these things in view and not be seduced away from what matters?

Most indigenous traditions, as Angeles Arrien discovered, uphold a practice of neither denying nor indulging the circumstances of life. This seems a useful guide. On the surface, this appears similar to the Buddhist notion of the Middle Way or the Christian value of moderation. But I think this points more to where we put our care and attention than to monitoring if we get too deeply involved. It speaks more to insuring that we give our full presence and effort to a place that remains authentic. It speaks, I think, to staying on course. And being human, we always veer off course. So, neither denying nor indulging are two human oars by which we can steer.

To see how this works, we only have to look at our relationship to fear and doubt. For denial uses fear to pull us out of life. It removes us from experience. And indulgence—not the sort whereby we eat the whole bag of cookies, but the kind that stalls us in one tension of living—such indulgence uses doubt and worry to keep us so entrenched in one aspect of our lives that we can't seem to move forward in the stream of life. The chance to know love is a perennial example. When a relationship is changing—that is, birthing or dying—and we deny the pain of that truth, we often thrust ourselves into a side life of denial, whereby we solicit misadventures, such as affairs or other addictions, to soothe the ache we carry rather than face things as they are. And yet an opposite response to the same situation can mire us in a painful journey of indulgence, whereby we endlessly process and circle the dysfunctions we've created rather than accept things as they are and repair or move on.

Somehow people have known for a long time that neither denying nor indulging our legitimate reactions to the world helps us maintain an accurate picture of the world and ourselves. Both—our ability to look when we need to and our ability to stop looking when we've over-analyzed the life out of our struggles—both form a crucial twin-skill. It seems that half of our work in a daily sense is to cut away what is false or distorted, finding what is true. The other half is then to be in authentic relationship with what is actually there.

These things are all tied to each other. When you lose hold of the thread of things as they are and find yourself busy turning one thing into another, ask yourself if you are denying some truth you need to look at, or if you are indulging some truth you need to act on. These questions are part of how we make things real.

## MAKING REAL

Realization means *making real*. In other words, it is a direct, immediate immersion into things as they absolutely are: no preconceptions, no interpretations, no judgment. It is oneself *becoming true*.

—GERALD MAY

During his walking pilgrimage around the island of Japan in the 1600s, Basho paused after a long day of hiking uphill and, before retiring, read these lines from his contemporary Hokushi:

> Hoping for beauty . . .
> he peers into the mask.

He looked out from the mountain into the twilight and felt something disturbing about Hokushi's insight when read aloud before the beauty of the Japanese sky. I imagine what jarred Basho was the understanding of how we continually look elsewhere for beauty rather than in the realities we are born to. How, through ideals and dreams and the search for perfection, we are seduced to see what we want to see instead of what is there. How we continually have the choice: whether to create beauty or to reveal beauty. How, not seeing the beauty in our own faces, we create masks, and how seeing things through a mask is what we call illusion. How we can then be distracted into striving for illusions and caring for masks. I imagine that Hokushi's small poem made Basho put down his own mask for a moment as he looked upon the beauty of the Japanese sky. We can ask no more of truth or love than to move us to pause and put down our mask.

Often, we put a mask on reality. We call these philosophies or worldviews. Here is one I cared for as a young man. When starting out, I read about the philosopher's stone and thought it a noble quest to try to take simple iron and find a way to turn it into gold. I spent long hours understanding it as a metaphor for the purpose of philosophy and art: to search for an alchemy that would turn the iron of the world into gold; not the bullion of wealth, but the essence that is worth preserving. Of course, being pummeled over decades into the beauty of things as they are, I now understand that it is all about realizing that the iron *is already* gold. I now feel certain that the true purpose of philosophy and art is to realize the gold already in everything by immersing ourselves directly and immediately into things as they are.

---

So, in an effort to keep these elusive things in view, let me suggest that one ongoing task of being a spirit in the world is to immerse ourselves directly into life and, thereby, make ourselves real. Crucial to that end is our ability to hold on to the thread of things as they are. But being human, we lose the thread, and one way to return to this ground of reality is to practice the fundamental request of all rest: to not turn one thing into another. Yet how do we do that? One age-old insight is to neither deny nor indulge the circumstances and feelings we encounter. This helps us maintain an accurate picture of the world and ourselves. Still, even at this level, how do we do this? By practicing when and how to look. For the workhorse of denial is fear, which is fueled by not looking when we need to. And the workhorse of indulgence is doubt, which is fueled by looking too much when we need to stop replaying what is before us and accept what is. Paradoxically, it all goes back to a devotion to things as they are. For therein lies the gold.

While these things appear in small ways, these are not small matters. For we have precious little time to become true and to make ourselves real. And it is often in the jagged edges of experience we refuse to pick up that the mystical strength of all human experience waits. In truth, any sliver of glass or broken dream will do to puncture our illusions. There, we will stumble on holy ground. For, as the medieval monk Meister Eckhart affirmed, "Is-ness is God."

# HEAVEN ON EARTH

Life is so full of meaning and purpose, so full of beauty
beneath its covering that you will find earth but cloaks your
heaven. Courage, then, to claim it, that is all. But courage we
have, and the knowledge that we are all pilgrims together,
wending through this unknown country, home.

—FRA GIOVANNI GIOCONDO,
*letter to a friend, 1513*

It's April and it's early. The sun is just rising and the tops of the
trees, not yet with leaves, are stretching into the warmth. They
seem to be awakening into a very slow dance. This might describe
joy. The sensation of awakening into a very slow dance. In this,
joy is different from happiness. While happiness might be the
momentary alignment of what we want with what happens, joy is
the fleeting, though slower, sense of feeling our connection to
everything with nothing in the way. While happiness might be
the peak feeling of release from pain or difficulty, joy is more the
immense promise of being alive that *holds* us in our pain or difficulty. For sure, happiness is as worthy as joy—for God's sake, turn
down neither! Yet, while happiness is the bud opening on the
branch, joy is feeling the entire tree—feeling the root lengthen as

the bud opens. And so joy is feeling Heaven on Earth. And April isn't the cruelest month, but the most promising.

So let's talk about joy. A few months ago, for my fifty-third birthday, Susan took me to a B.B. King concert. It made me both happy and joyous. B.B. King and his music are part of the musical sky of my life. And there he was, seventy-five years old, diabetic, shuffling onstage with those bad knees. Shuffling to a simple folding chair where his guitar, Lucille, was waiting. I've always loved that B.B. named his guitar. In a very subtle way, it gave me permission as a young man to love objects and to see the life in them. As the music began, though he was sitting the entire time, his body couldn't sit still. Each rhythm poked another corner of his soul and he, as if tickled or caressed, would jump and sigh.

Just watching him made me happy. As I looked around in the concert light, I saw Susan's opened face, which I love to watch, and the hearts of strangers relaxing in the dark. And I realized there were hundreds of us coming out of our modern caves, parking in the rain, and waiting on line—all for B.B. to show us how to feel music, even when you can't stand up. In that sudden opened moment, I felt something that was mine and not mine, something that was both in me and between me and everyone there. Even the broken statue on the ceiling was leaning into us. For the moment, I stopped smiling, for the smile was too deep. I had fallen into a moment of joy.

I used to think that the reward for knowing truth was wisdom, and in some ways, it is. But more deeply, if we can *enter* truth, the reward is joy. Indeed, joy lives *inside* the blues. And you have to *sing* them open, so the joy can fly out. This is why holding things in is so dangerous. We are human instruments and experience plucks our strings and our feelings are the notes. If we don't sing them open, they build up and batter the heart from the inside out—till we explode. So it's never been about singing well, just singing. This is the difference between entertainment and staying alive. This is

B.B.'s true gift. Of course, he's a master musician, but underneath that, he is a master at singing the blues, at feeling truth until it opens to joy—a master at staying alive. This is what every oppressed people, at the heart of their music and poetry and story and art, have to teach us.

I remember my first step after surgery, after having that rib removed from my back. Never had a step been so painful and pointed and so miraculous and supporting. I even felt the air beneath my heel cushion my sorry weight to the ground. That moment, beyond explanation, was a moment of joy. I saw it as well in South Africa, in the face of a boy in a side street of Cape Town. After flying twenty-two hours and losing all sense of day or night, I was wandering the city when I came upon a circle of boys clapping and tapping their feet. Once close enough to see the center of their circle, I saw a twelve-year-old dancing around his crutch.

The Sufi poet Ghalib declared that "for the raindrop, joy is entering the lake." Indeed, isn't this the purpose of searching, to become one with things? And isn't joy, then, the sensation that overcomes us as we experience Oneness? And let's talk about peace. A contemporary poet, Elizabeth Goldman, remarks that "peace is a sensation, a cup resting in its given sphere." Isn't this the purpose of being? Isn't peace, then, a feeling of true placement, a sense of arriving in moments of right relationship to the universe, when we fit lightly and securely into the space of our lives?

The truth is that living within ourselves within the Whole leads us to a humility of being. And lifting our eyes in such a mood of being not only welcomes us into the nature of things as they are, but such a humility awakens a heightened sensibility of heart and mind that ushers us into the province of Heaven on Earth.

Joseph Campbell profoundly speaks of it this way:

For those who have found the still point of eternity, around which all—including themselves—revolves, everything is acceptable as it is; indeed, can be experienced as glorious and wonderful. The first duty of the individual, consequently, is simply to play their given role—as do the sun and moon, the various animal and plant species, the waters, the rocks, and the stars—without resistance, without fault; and then, if possible, so to order their mind as to identify its consciousness with the inhabiting principle of the whole.

Such a moment, for me, was with Grandma when I was a boy. I realize now that her love was pointing me to God. I was eight or nine, rummaging through her basement, through my dead grandfather's books, and she appeared at the foot of the old see-through stairs, nostalgic that I should be searching through his things. There were no windows, and the only light came flooding down the length of stairs over her massive shoulders, giving a sheen to her mat of gray hair. When I turned, she seemed an immigrant deity. I ran to her with this relic, so worn that the cover was indented with a palm print, the edges crumbling like petrified wood. The book seemed very mysterious. The letters were not even in English but in strange and beautiful configurations. She almost cried and sat on the bottom step. I snuggled between her legs, against her apron. She gathered me in as she opened the relic and said, "This was your grandfather's Talmud. He brought it from Russia." I remember running my little hands all over it the way I do large boulders, trying to feel the years of wind and rain. Her hands were huge and worked, like movable stones themselves. She turned me by the shoulders and, with the light flooding my face, she whispered, more firmly than I had ever heard anyone whisper, "You are why we came to this country. . . ." She took me by the chin. "You are why I live." She put the relic in my small hands. I was tentative. She gripped me to it firmly and my small palm slid into the well of my grandfather's touch. She stood on the bottom step, blocking the light. "I love you like life itself." She reached down and sandwiched my little fingers. "These are the oldest things you own." As she waddled up the stairs, the light wavered on and off my face. Without turning, she went back to her kitchen. I stood and the light settled in the impression of Nehemiah's grip, a man I never knew, and I didn't want to leave this dungy threshold. I was afraid to climb back into the light. I stood before those stairs, a grimy little innocent, and felt like an orphan who'd been told I was a prince to a kingdom that had perished before I was born. I leafed through the strange letters, watching the light make glitter of the dust. I put the book behind a secret shelf, afraid it would crumble if brought into the world, and walked the lighted stairs, taller than I had descended. I entered her kitchen older yet still a child and climbed her lap like a throne.

In that moment I experienced the still point of eternity, and everything in that basement seemed glorious for what it was. I had no need to change it, to turn it into anything else. I also had no language for it. But climbing back into the world, I carried that moment and its peace and its joy with me—through basketball and first loves and college insanities and marriages and cancer. It is still with me. And now I know that one indication that I am near Heaven on Earth is that the smallest details carry everything. My friend Rob Lehman has wisely concluded that "the heart's experience of Wholeness is the radical awareness that each part contains the Whole." As a boy that day I knew this. My grandfather's Talmud, the light through Grandma's legs, her large hands holding mine—each of these fragments of ordinary life contained everything.

Of course, it's hard to access that still point when in crisis or depressed, hard to believe that "Earth but cloaks your Heaven" when feeling broken by loss or grief. But it is misleading to think that joy and peace are only available when we are happy or quiet.

Just as food is the only thing that will keep us alive when starving, joy and peace are the things that will keep us alive when we are lost and suffering—if we can find them.

I'm reminded of a reluctant elder of the Kovno Ghetto in Nazi-occupied Lithuania. He was a humble and brilliant physician, Elkhanan Elkes. He was chosen by his people to deal with the Nazis because, while they bickered over who should be their leader, he was the only one left whom everyone could trust. It was a difficult tenure, and after more than a year of unspeakable betrayals and brutalities, the dwindling Ghetto was facing certain, if unpredictable, death. And so Dr. Elkes convened a symphony that rehearsed and performed concerts for those still alive. In the face of certain death with nothing to do, they devoted themselves to opening eternity in whatever moments were left. They devoted themselves to having nothing in the way; to peeling away both the past and the future; to opening the one impregnable feeling of wholeness hiding in the music. And this mysterious moment of Heaven on Earth covered them briefly with joy and peace as they approached their death.

It is the same for us all, though thankfully not as dire. No matter the pain or complication we face, we can devote ourselves to removing whatever is in the way. We can peel away the past and the future, and open the invincible moment that encompasses everything, wherever we may find it. And the joy and peace found there will cover us briefly—if we can let it in.

Still, this all can be confusing. For the deeper we go, the more feelings merge. And since joy is the culminating feeling of wholeness, it contains all our emotions and can show its face through any one. This is why it is difficult sometimes to distinguish a feeling of depth from sadness. Is it sadness we're feeling or the pure ache of being alive that the pain of some loss has opened? Is it sadness we're feeling or the ache of feeling nothing in the way, an ache that *includes* our sadness? In a moment of love for another, is it our love for that person alone that overwhelms us or has that love *opened* a deeper love for the very air that cushions our sorry weight to the ground? Often, it is both. For it seems that, as we grow in the life of Spirit, we are asked to apprentice at living with this heightened sensibility of heart and mind, where we encounter poignancies that are greater and deeper than any one feeling. They are the awakened feelings of the raindrop entering the river and of the cup resting in its given sphere.

So, when we find ourselves unable to distinguish between feelings, when feelings start to occur simultaneously, we are close to that jarring threshold of Heaven on Earth. Now it makes sense to look through our sadness to see if that ache of being alive is underneath it. Now it makes sense to look through our confusion and doubt to see if we are starting to feel wholeness by embracing more than one feeling at the same time.

In living it, this feeling-things-so-deeply-that-they-carry-more-than-one-face can be confusing, but when we can stay with it, we are privileged to find that this is where things are joined. And whenever we begin to sense where things are joined, there the cloak is parted—there we begin to sense Heaven on Earth.

The Buddhist monk Thich Nhat Hanh speaks to this when he says:

> One thing is made up of all other things. One thing contains the whole cosmos. . . . A piece of bread contains sunshine through a cloud . . . Without the sun or cloud, the wheat cannot grow. So when you eat a piece of bread, you eat the cloud, you eat the sunshine, you eat the minerals, time, space, everything.

Recently, I experienced a small moment of this. It is still very much with me. After a day of writing, and a day of Susan working at the potter's wheel, she and I curl on the couch and our dog-child, Mira, comes over with her pooling eyes. We ask if she wants to come up, and she hops on the couch and drapes herself in the folds of our legs, snuggling between us as much as possible. And the three of us sigh and watch the day turn to night as small birds announce themselves and fly, their soft songs outlasting the day. By now we have listened so closely that we feel something of our peace rise with their songs into the dying light till all that's left of us or them are pins of light that we, for lack of a better name, call stars. I look at Susan and Mira, feel them both, feel the birds, the night, their song, our peace, feel the stars that hold us all in place, feel them cushion us as we breathe. As we sigh, they flicker, our breath and their light tugging at each other. We have fallen through. This is Heaven on Earth. This quiet sensation of everything being so fully in place that it aches—this is joy.

# AT THE PACE OF
# WHAT IS REAL

*If courageous enough, we might
just slow to the pace of creation,
where the pulse by which the mind thinks
touches the pulse by which the heart feels,
and together they equal the rhythm of miracle:
where being plays in exact motion
with all being.*

There is much talk of being present and entering the moment. It is highly valued in our time as an antidote to the tensions of the modern world. And rightly so. Some forty years ago, Ram Dass clearly rang the ancient bell when he shouted, "Be here now!" For all traditions sanctify the moment, not merely as a medicine to quell the symptoms of an agitated life, but more deeply as a perennial doorway to the company of the Whole.

Yet what does it mean to enter the moment? And what conditions of inwardness open the moment before us? We've looked at this from many vantage points. Still, there is one more to consider. It has to do with aligning the pace at which we think with the pace at which we feel. This seems to empower a deeper means of seeing and knowing the world. Like tumblers in a lock, when the pace of true thinking aligns with the pace of authentic feeling, and when these in turn align with a seeing and hearing that returns us to a freshness of first perception—the moment clicks open. The hidden wholeness is unlocked.

More often than not, we have to *slow* our thinking and feeling and seeing and hearing until they open into each other. Once there, a common rhythm of being appears, which we can call the pace of creation. And the effort to enter each moment in this way is living at the pace of what is real.

It is interesting that when a Navajo elder was asked to define healing, he spoke of *Ahyo-oh'-oh-ni*, which is Navajo for "to bring one into harmony with everything." As well, the psychiatrist Gerald May has remarked that "realness is the ground of true confidence," which is a Western way of saying the same thing. For true confidence at its fundamental core is the realness or authority of presence that comes from being brought into harmony with everything.

Entering the moment is the most direct way we have of doing this. How? By entering each particular before us. How? By slowing our thinking and feeling and seeing and hearing to the pace of creation. How? By preserving and following the breath that joins us to the things around us. Here we are brought into harmony with everything. Such realness opens us to the greater motion of all being that we are always a part of.

I just had a great teaching in this regard. But in order to share this, I need to trace some events of the last year. You see, next week will be a year since we moved to Michigan. Of the many things we boxed and packed, we took an old wooden bench which sat on the edge of our garden in upstate New York. It is a small, unpainted bench that was there when we moved in; crudely made with two wide boards for legs and a third board nailed in various ways as a seat. The seat is split and can pop up, if you're not careful. We had it in front of a large forsythia bush. The bench feels more ancient than it seems, like a relic from some medieval monastery. Anyway, we now live on a hill, and last year, as soon as it was warm enough, we put the bench under a canopy of oak trees near the house. It was a magical spot that seemed to bridge our past and our present.

It wasn't long till spring was in full bloom and we discovered quiet trails along the shores of nearby Lake Michigan, a magnificent lake that feels like a freshwater ocean. And so we spent hours walking the dunes there with our dog, Mira, she playing with the small surf, while we held rounded stones, wondering what they might say had they the chance. It was toward the end of summer, when no one was around, that we found this smooth, bleached bough with one equally smooth branch forking off one end. It seemed important, like a wooden flute that had lost its holes to the erosion of the sea. We took it home and, unsure what we were supposed to do with it, carefully leaned it in a corner of the garage.

Soon after this, my dear friend Robert sent us an unusual housewarming present—an oar! It was a meaningful surprise that traced back to the Jungian analyst Helen Luke. Both Robert and I regard Helen as a mentor, and it was her interpretation of Ulysses' vision as an old man that taught us both about starting anew. It was long after the Trojan War, after the ten-year Odyssey home, after the freeing of his wife, Penelope, in Ithaka. Ulysses was getting restless, itching to go back to sea, where he was regarded as a master. He was ready to go—to refind his glory—when the soothsayer Tieresias came to him in a vision and said, "No—you shall keep walking *inland* until you meet someone who doesn't even know what an oar is. There, you shall plant the oar and start a garden."

And so Robert gave us an oar. That first winter we put the old bench in the basement, left the driftwood in the garage along with a glider needing to be assembled, and the oar was in the house, looking lonely without a boat. During the winter, we listened to the winds move about the hill.

Then things began to thaw, and last week we had an unusually warm day. The daffodils were budding. So we assembled the glider in the driveway as our dog kept stealing the instructions. Finally, we put it together and it now seemed obvious that it belonged under the canopy of oak trees where the bench had been. So we started looking for a new place for the old bench.

I carried the bench up the hill to the highest corner, where I had traipsed in the snow to glimpse the moon. Sure enough, we found a spot that seemed almost magnetic. The bench wanted to be there. I thought just to leave it, but noticed that the ground, of course, wasn't level. So I dug out a small landing. Then, as I started to walk away, the cut-out upper half of the circle and the mounded lower half were begging for stones. We had a pile we'd been stacking since moving in. I carried them over and on my knees began packing and petting the heavy stones in place.

By this time, Susan had bought a forsythia and we planted it near the bench. But the hill was calling for something else. So, after lunch, we bought four bags of pea gravel and some marble chips. And I began to cover the landing with a floor of pebbles, bordering the stone circle with marble.

As we backed off the hill, we looked at this perch that had somehow appeared through our unexpected efforts. It seemed holy and oracle-like. Then we both realized why we had picked up the driftwood. We pulled it from the garage and planted it behind the landing, hanging wooden chimes on the lone bleached branch. Now we knew where to put the oar. And so we carried it together and planted it, handle in the earth, on the uppermost crest of the hill.

I was struck by how all these simple and seemingly unrelated things—bench, driftwood, oar, pea gravel—drew us to them. And how each was a clue to discovering this holy spot that was there all along, waiting through that long first winter for us to make it visible.

The next night was mild, and along around midnight, I took Mira out, then climbed the hill to sit on the bench. The moon was full, the stars were clear. Tufts of clouds were drifting across the big, ancient sky. The breeze was quietly rattling the tops of the still-leafless trees. It felt like Eden. I don't know how long I sat there, but my heart was stunned. Inadvertently, we had uncovered a timeless nook from which to watch the magnitude of the earth. I had the same stunned feeling when walking beyond the tree line in the Rockies, when listening to the Pacific early in the morning, and when looking back at Cape Town, at the very bottom of Africa, from the Indian Ocean.

Always, the things we hold, the things we water in place, the small moments we open—all are quiet steps that can lead us to some view of eternity. Now I think the magnitude of love, peace, wisdom, and truth can be known like this. For they are there all along, waiting to be discovered—all vast planes of being like sky, ocean, and mountains, waiting to be entered moment by moment. Clearly, by living at the pace of what is real, we can access the vitalities that matter. And though everything conspires to move us ahead of this pace—pain, fear, loss, doubt, anxiety, ambition—we can recover the pace of creation by slowing to where all things begin.

I first understood this in the tender months after chemo ended. I was drifting in a rowboat writing a letter to my father, who thought I sounded different. And I did. Here is part of that letter:

You ask if anything's changed. I write this in an open boat in the middle of a lake which has been drawing me to its secret for months. I am becoming more like water by the day. The slightest brace of wind stirs me through. I am more alive than ever.

What does that mean? That in the beginning I was awakened as if a step behind, always catching up, as if waking in the middle of some race that started before I arrived, waking to all these frantic strangers hurrying me on, as if landing in the middle of some festival not knowing what to celebrate, as if someone genuine and beautiful had offered to love me just before I could hear and now I must find them.

You ask if anything's changed. I am drifting in the lake and now it's a matter of slowing so as not to pass it by.

That was almost fifteen years ago. Now, when I slow down, I am drawn to life's clues. For entering into relationship with these small and simple things opens the bird's call. By slowing down, the wind makes an old tree whisper, and the light makes a broken piece of glass glisten with truth, and a drop of rain somehow makes the eye of a fly as soft as someone tired of running.

I'm writing this on the moon bench toward the end of a quiet day, very slowly, a word at a time. The oar is over my shoulder, planted firmly in the ground. And I'm waiting for what speaks when the wind through the chimes, and the clouds, and my breath all exhale at the same time.

# IN FLAWED ABUNDANCE

The abundance of life is always present. When we recognize
it, it opens our consciousness . . . and it comes flowing in mind
and body with a mighty, quickening, healing power that
renews, transforms, and changes.

—CHARLES FILLMORE

As I sit in the sun years later, I realize it was during such a
moment in a hospital room, recovering from surgery, barely able
to walk, that I was surprised to discover that everything we need
or want is waiting inside each day. It seems impossible, a riddle of
living, but everything we need is right before us in flawed abundance.

I was bringing a glass of water slowly to my lips, when the light
through the dusty window rushed through the glass, and I could
see all the impurities, an entire world barely swirling in the clear-
ness. It made me realize that nothing is clean or perfect, and nothing unfolds as planned. For the Universe is vital, not perfect. Full
of endless seeds attempting to be one thing, colliding with
another, and becoming a third. Loves, dreams, difficulties, peace
of mind—all of who we are unfolds this way beyond our willful
wanting. I said amen and drank the water and felt it join me further
with the world.

I later read that in the Aramaic language that Jesus spoke, the King James phrase "be you perfect" really means "be you all-embracing." It's a misinterpretation that changes everything. For the goal is not to sift the thousand things held to the light, but to drink them.

My own life is a clear example. I didn't want cancer. I didn't want to stop teaching. But I so wanted to live and was forced to keep learning. I didn't want to be still or slow down. But was forced by pain to fall into the peace and wonder that stillness and silence opens.

Much of our unhappiness comes from insisting on what we want as the only path to contentment. Often, beyond what we want is what we need, waiting in the abundance of a reality that has more than enough to keep us vital and alive. In truth, life has an intricate and dazzling order that defies the grasp of any mind, and so, from the limits of our thinking, we often call it messy. Likewise, life has an abundance of unexpected gifts that surprises our narrow definition of success, and so, from our narrow focus, we often dismiss these gifts as obstacles, because they don't seem to pertain to what we want. Yet, ultimately, when we pretend to know what we need, we preclude all cross-pollination and cut ourselves off from being seeded by all the colors that are not us.

One of the more difficult paradoxes to accept is that this abundance of gifts is always quietly present and that it is *we* who drift in and out of seeing it. The one recurring doorway to this vitality is our simple participation in life. When we slip into heartless watching, the abundance seems to vanish. When we dare to show up and be fully present, grace and wonder and mystery start to appear, even in the midst of pain. Not as planned dreams, or as images of lovers, or as scripts of success designed by our fantasies of ourselves. But as oddly shaped pods of vitality bursting to multiply and bring us further into the mystery of living.

It seems obvious but worth saying that being removed from the life of our own experience jeopardizes our sense of belonging to a Universe that is thriving and larger than our problems. Ironically, people have tried for ages to quarantine themselves from the wheel of life and all the sounds it makes as it turns. It's too scary. It's too dreary. It's overwhelming. It makes me feel so insignificant. Which all may be true. But it's leaning *into* the truth of what happens that heals us by opening the fabric of life that holds all this. In actuality, there is no life outside the life of experience.

As Aldous Huxley wisely says:

It is through self-knowledge, not through belief in somebody else's symbols, that a person comes to the eternal reality, in which their being is grounded.

It is important to note here that attention alone is not a passport to wellness or peace. There is something else that is crucial. After all, Hitler's operatives devoted enormous attention to the killing of eleven million human beings. So, attention by itself, like any tool, can be used or misused. Consider how we exert endless attention in guarding ourselves against misfortune. Though sometimes necessary, this is hardly enlightening. It is, in fact, quite draining. How tiring to sleep with one eye open, vigilant not to be robbed. Still, being alert is different from moving toward what is precious.

There is a painful difference between *fear-based attention* and *trust-based attention*. A tiring difference between a vigilance of mind that doesn't want to be taken advantage of and an attention of heart that longs to belong to all that is enlivening. This brings us back to sincerity, and it's interesting that in the Aramaic language that Jesus spoke, the word *peshitta* means "simple, sincere, and true." Interesting that our flaws, when not hidden, are the simple, sincere, and true cracks that other life can fill, the way light fills a shadow or water fills a hole.

Perhaps it is our humanness that helps us find each other. Perhaps it is precisely because we are not perfect that we can complete each other. Perhaps it is through our flaws and shortcomings that the abundance of life streams its gifts as it constantly rebalances the Universe, the way water always finds its level. Perhaps, as the great educator Parker Palmer says, "the major failures of our time are not ethical failures but failures of human wholeness."

I do know that when I stop replaying the events of my life, I can hear the trees push back their bark. And then I realize that all the buried seeds crack open in the dark the instant they surrender to a process they can't see.

So yes, it is true. I confess. I am one of the lighted impurities swirling in the glass. And I have thought great thoughts, and sung great songs—all of it rehearsal for the majesty of being held. For the years have forced me to surrender to a process I can't see. Now my efforts turn from trying to outrun suffering to accepting love wherever I can find it. Stripped of causes and plans and things to strive for, I have discovered that we cannot eliminate hunger, but we can feed each other. We cannot eliminate loneliness, but we can hold each other. We cannot eliminate pain, but we can live a life of compassion.

Ultimately, we are small living things awakened in the flawed, abundant stream, not gods who carve out rivers. Like human fish, we are asked to experience meaning in the life that moves through the gill of our heart. Ultimately, there is nothing to do and nowhere to go. Accepting this, we can do everything and go anywhere.

# THE MYSTERIOUS PRESS
# OF ONENESS

*Dancers while dancing
drape all they know around it,
and children while laughing
let their laughter praise it,
and my heart breaks open as
strangers flower their love
through the breaks
in their strangeness.*

All along, we've been describing being human as a humble condition in which we keep falling in and out of achieving and blossoming, in and out of arriving and being, and in and out of thinking that destiny is a movement from now to when, only to realize it is more an awakening from inner to outer.

What is it, then, that opens us and returns us to this interior sense of destiny? I know that, for me, when I chance to be honest, I stumble into the sacred. When I am pried open long enough, I become vulnerable and compassionate. And when I dare to express whatever is being pressed through me, no matter how awkward or subtle my expression, some ever-present wind enlivens me. The Navajo call this enlivening press of Oneness *Nilchi*—"the holy wind that informs everything."

I confess that I have known that holy wind, from time to time, and I have come to understand that the same qualities of honesty, compassion, and expression that are required to face death and to survive illness are the very same qualities required to live our ordinary days. From here, we are given many chances to learn how to love and how to face things, both of which seem so frightening and monumental at first, but which become inevitable teachers and friends, when we can admit them.

Once we find our way to being awake, the work of being a spirit in the world is to stay awake. Often, we need each other to discover how. There is an old South African proverb that says that the reason two antelope walk together is so that one can blow the dust from the other's eyes. This sort of friendship enables joy. And joy, too, is our destiny: the feeling of Oneness that, while we're in it, never falls short.

But in order to feel Oneness, we are drawn into another kind of struggle: the pain of expanding our sense of self beyond our personal boundaries into the heart of a humanity that includes everyone, a humanity that is timeless. This is another archetypal journey. And while we can easily conjure up examples of people confined to their smaller, egocentric worlds, as well as those humbled into a waking compassion for all life, the transformation from one to the other—from the agitation of our personal concerns to the swelling sea of Oneness—can be difficult and unclear.

Many experiences can trigger this—a great idea that jars our tidy sense of things, or the loss of someone we thought we would love forever, or the quiet power of dew on a peony. Suddenly, there is a terrible tension between the boundaries of our personal self and the experience of a Universal self. Suddenly, it is no longer clear where we live: in here or out there. And the in-between time, when the chambers of the heart are still accepting that it is both, can be crazy-making.

You see, the rush of life's energy flooding through our tiny, singular self can make us feel confused, unsure if everything is breaking down or opening up, unsure if we are losing everything or gaining everything. This is the baptism of becoming porous. And the tension of being both your self and part of something larger than your self leads us right into the heart of a profound paradox, captured beautifully by St. Bonaventure when he says that "God is a circle whose center is everywhere and whose circumference is nowhere."

I was thrown into this confusing tension two years ago. I was staying with friends on the edge of a canyon in Sante Fe. And early, before dawn, I was awakened by the howl of a coyote. It seemed piercing and close. Without turning on the light, I went to the window and peered through the blinds. In a blue cast of moonlight, there were two scraggly creatures about twenty feet from the house. The larger one was standing perfectly still, its head pointing skyward in a continual howl. The smaller one was calmly grazing behind it. Together they seemed complete.

I sat at my friend's desk in the dark and there, tacked to her wall, were two handwritten quotes I'd never noticed. Both spoke of the center and the circumference, and of how to proceed in the world. The first, by Buddha, spoke of the center: "Act always as if the future of the Universe depends on what you do, while laughing at yourself for thinking that whatever you do makes any difference." The second, by Nietzsche, spoke of the circumference: "I want to learn more and more to see as beautiful what is necessary in things, then I shall be one of those who makes things beautiful."

The larger coyote began to howl forcefully. I peered again through the blinds and, suddenly, it seemed as if these two were scraggly angels sent to wake me to these teachings. And there I was, in the desert night, in my underwear, reading and watching, again and again, until it seemed that the coyotes were voicing the quotes. It made me name them. Of course, the howling one was Nietzsche and the grazing one was Buddha. I watched and laughed at myself. How much it takes, sometimes, for me to wake.

After a while, I fell back asleep. In the morning, they were gone. I've carried the coyote quotes as a koan ever since.

For how do we see what is necessary as beautiful? How do we make a difference with humility? I'm not sure I know. I'm just living into it. But this is the mysterious press of Oneness. How do we bring the center to bear on the circumference? How do we move from the lip of the source through our dear but tiny souls all the way to the tip of our hands meeting the world? How do we no longer pit good against bad, in a fight that never seems to end, and just let what is awake inform what is not? Perhaps Nietzsche and Buddha are guides. For wherever we live, the effort to see what is necessary as beautiful and to make a difference with humility just might bring the source and the world—the center and the circumference—together through us.

# CHORES

―――――――――〜〜―――――――――

*It all bares down to something vital*
*that moves through everything,*
*and when we recognize it,*
*we feel the place that no one*
*can hold and know*
*we are home.*

As sticks were rubbed prehistorically to start fires, the rubbing of our humanity against what is daily sparks the spiritual. This quiet discovery is as important as the wheel. For tedious as it might be to fix the broken hoe so you can rake the earth, it is this involvement that saves us. As the Lakota have said for generations, "Tell me and I will forget. Show me and I will remember. Involve me and I will understand." And so it is no accident that the things of this world break down, involving us in their mending. It is our best chance, as stubborn creatures, to live and understand.

I confess I used to hate chores. As a young man, I was obsessed with creating. I had no patience for fixing or maintaining, largely because I was surrounded by those equally obsessed with fixing, so much so that they seldom experienced anything new. Or so it seemed to me. They seldom leaned into the unplanned joy of discovery. They seemed obligated to fix everything, prompted by some constant worry or low-grade fear. But beyond all this, I really had no use for the earthly life. I was instinctively a mystic, and mistaken in thinking that life was somewhere other than here. I kept waiting for the vibrancy of the world to blow through the veils of appearance, and so I only wanted to live on the other side.

But the years have made it clear that this distinction existed in *me*. In truth, the elusive quality of life that I was chasing was the result of *my* inability to stay involved. Clearly my eyes have been rearranged, for now I find spirit *in everything*. It's as if what matters has melted into the thousand objects that make up the days, the way snow melts into the earth. Accepting this, my sense of joy has taken root in the thousand things I encounter.

I've come to understand that the wonder of being transformed is living more coherently *within one's self*. For just as the world surrounding a fetus does not change, though what it senses changes dramatically as it forms its eyes, is born, first opens them, and finally sees—it is *we* who change. And once on the other side of such change, only a buffoon would insist that the nature of the Universe has shifted. Clearly, I've become more integrated, forming new eyes. Clearly, my spirit has more thoroughly joined my body, birthing a different me. Clearly, who I am has melted more completely into the ordinary fact of my days.

Yes, my ideals and fantasies of life, once purely written in the sky, have melted, soaking like water into the even more glorious dirt. More glorious because such an earthly involvement breaks down the false separation of ideas from experience. More glorious because such an ordinary involvement softens the withdrawal and transcendence by which the lonely and intelligent often try to remove themselves from the messy abundance of what is.

So now I do the chores I used to hate, disliking them until my immersion takes me beneath the silhouette of mind that knows it as a chore, in much the way that saying the word *wind* long enough strips it of all familiarity. In this way, I do the chores slowly with full attention; tinkering, maintaining, fixing; doing all the things I vowed I wouldn't.

Just today I found myself stepping through mounds of silage piled before the stanchions in a barn, because the door to the manure-filled pen would no longer close. The barn had shifted over the years and the door was sticking on the concrete sill. I put hay on the manure around the door and knelt with a saw, trying to cut the bottom of the door by half an inch. At first I didn't want to do it, but there I was, caught in the motion of sawing horizontally. I could hear the cows chewing as the saw gained its rhythm. I kept watching the saw's teeth rip further and further across the bottom of the door. And though wood cannot feel, at least not as we feel, or so we think, when pushing the saw faster than it could easily cut, I felt violent. When backing off and letting the saw glide in its own stroke, I felt so inside the sensation of sawing a door free that I could have been a carpenter planing Solomon's gate.

The day's earthiness returned, though it had never disappeared. As I stood, my knees were wet with manure and the door swung freely over a sliver of daylight through which the wind was now curling. I wondered if that sheet of air would chill the cows. I was amazed at how much light that sliver of wood let in.

It made me wonder: How do *we* shift over the years? How are our foundations eaten away? When beaten by the weather of living, how rough are we in the opening? And what, then, is the saw but the work of honest love: kneeling in our own manure or the manure of others, holding the broken gate firmly, and letting our honesty rip slowly in its stroke across the bottom of our door. All this till a sliver of light pours through, even when the door is closed; till we know ourselves by what shines through, even when we are closed.

I went into the house and collected all the garbage that would burn and lugged it to the rusty old barrel beyond the apple trees. There was something profound in this simplicity of carting used

containers and old newspapers to the burning barrel. They lit easily, yellow flames opening like little shawls. I watched the cello-
phane that carried the perch all frozen from the sea. It dissolved to
a clear shimmer that rose, as if the last motion of that fish rising for
its hook was now being released. I watched the stories of brutality
merge into smoke, saw the face of a missing child collapse into
flame. Saw the list of numbers curl, the ones we kept by the phone
while Helen was dying, saw her doctor's -2473 unlink and char.
Saw it all rise in a clear flame that softened the sky.

After lunch, I looked for something to fix and settled on the
bluebird houses, whose openings must face south. They must
stand alone at the edge of a field or the birds will never show. In
order to fasten them to fence posts, I tried to hammer new boards
to the backs of the old houses. The hammering was delicate: too
hard and the worn houses fell apart, not hard enough and the
backings wouldn't hold. I used old nails. They seemed more pli-
able. The houses once cleaned and backed were a bit rickety, but I
trudged to the far end of the cow field and nailed them up as the
cows thundered away. I stood and watched the oldest house pick
up the wind, heard it enter the little bluebird hole and whip
around inside.

I felt the wind whip through me and thought, How much of our
tiny lives is obsessed with shutting out and letting in. How we
build and burn by turns. How we make things fit to keep the wind
out. How we make things loose to let the light in. How much we
like hinges so we can change our mind. And what made us ever
think that building a small box with a little round hole would lure
something blue to fly down from the sky? Why would something
so free in the heavens seek such a confining home? And what
strange paradox makes it hold true?

We are returned to the question: Is it that all existence is part of
a balanced unity which flows from every part now full to every
part now empty? Or is it that the bluebird in its divine innocence

lives a wisdom we struggle to maintain: that the air behind the hole of the bluebird house is the same as the air in the heavens? And if so, is it our task, then, to regain the innocence of the bluebird until we, too, can realize that the air behind the hole in our heart is the same as the air that fills the Universe? Until, through our innocence and courage, we live out our freedom to move between the Universe within and the Universe without?

The houses must face south, the way the little hole in a person's heart must face toward truth, the way each of us must prop ourselves up in the open, our perforated heart open to the wind. And there, we must wait beyond all logic for something to fly out of the heavens and build its nest within us.

# WE BECOME THE EARTH

*In seeking what is essential,*
*we become essential.*

I have always been amazed how the deepest things are intangible: love, doubt, faith, confusion, peace. Where are they? They can't be held in the hand like fruit or turned in the lap like pages of a sacred text. Yet they shape our lives. This has always been the driving mystery of all sacred wisdom: The only things worth saying are those things that are unsayable.

It is quite humbling to realize that we spend a lifetime gaining grain after grain of this wisdom, working to understand it and struggling to express it, only to become more and more a part of it, unspeakable ourselves. Over time, we age into a stillness that breathes like stone, exposed beyond resistance.

Perhaps this is the most poignant of paradoxes, nature's safe-guard against letting too much of the mystery out. We take years of living to squeeze a few precious words from all that will not speak, and steadily, being shaped by our suffering and polished by our joy, we become the earth, knowing more and saying less. Ironically, after a lifetime, we may finally have important things to say, just as we lose our ability to say them. Yet this doesn't diminish all we try to say. For the fact that sound always ends in silence doesn't make music any less precious.

It seems the more we live through, the less we can surface. Again, I recall visiting Grandma Minnie when she was ninety-four. I've mentioned her several times. This time I had found the steamship ticket with which she came to this country in 1912 as a girl. There was a strange and beautiful name on it, Maiyessca. This was her birth name, never spoken in this country. I put the yellowed ticket in her hand. Her eyes widened and I could feel the big old fish of her heart swim up near the surface, stirring waters that had been still for eighty years. Lifetimes passed between us in silence. She trembled and coughed up a chuckle, saying only, "I forgot I ever came."

This is more profound than sad. Rather, it feels inevitable and holy that we should become what we seek. We start out wanting to know God, and suffering and loving long enough, we become a part of God. Over time, the heart expands while our skin thins until we become something elemental, rounding to the next grain of wisdom to be found.

As I age, I grow more and more clear inwardly as my joints start to creak. I was taken aback recently, when joining a fitness club, at the history of my body: a rib removed, torn ligaments in an ankle, torn muscle in a knee, torn meniscus in the other knee, arthritic thumbs, a skull bone worn thin by a tumor. At first I felt battered, but smiled to realize that I stand like a small cliff worn full of holes in which stray birds nest and I wake with the dreams they have while resting in me. In truth, each question carried over a lifetime is like a hole worn in a stone which held to the wind finally sings.

Early on, there is such wonder in the search, and wonder is still so much a part of my days, but there is, within the peace and joy of each wakeful moment, a small loneliness that comes from knowing and feeling much more than can ever be said. It is a curious wearing down that is both a vanishing and the making of a jewel.

And somehow this happens between generations as well. We utter what we can, trying to pass on what matters, only to have our children assume what we have earned—their rightful starting point. It makes me wonder, when my father dies, if all the things he couldn't say will fly out of him. If, like a butterfly's wing in the dark of another continent, the things he couldn't face will mount as a wind a thousand miles away. I wonder if his gifts will leave him, too. If his ability to build something out of nothing will spark another's confidence.

I know I was born to say what he couldn't, to face what he's turned from. It's the way these things work. An ecology of spirit. For instance, a friend has a little girl just ten months old, and I can tell by her deep attention that she's been here before. I can tell she will say what I cannot and face what I can't bear.

She stares at me and I stare back, our eyes sorting what lives, what breathes, what gives to the air. She still smells the womb-sea, and I, the rocks of this world. She's eager to be here, though her eyes don't understand the many shades of weight. But I feel compelled to translate weights, which means I sense the things that hide in wood and stone, the things that boil in the pot of human traffic.

How I make hymns of my father's pain. How my friend's little girl will make portraits of how I burn. This is necessary. It's how spirit recycles. We each are born one step closer to God than those we are born to, for which we are loved by some and never forgiven by others. We each will die with one more thing to say. We each will wake with something familiar on our lip, which we must find and love.

# BEING AND FEELING

*Yet when I stop,*
*it appears to me briefly*
*that life is just a dance*
*around a still point, which*
*knowing is a joy and*
*refusing is a burden.*

Much of my life has been devoted to understanding being and feeling. If pressed, I would have to say that all that understanding has given way to the realization that *to enter my experience* of being and feeling is how I know my soul. In essence, understanding has given way to embodiment. Insight has given way to presence. For sure, understanding and insight are still valuable, but after all the study and all the degrees, I truly get it: They serve the awakening of spirit and presence, not the other way around. Too much time is lost, and wasted, in pursuing wisdom over joy. Still, here is what I've learned.

To begin with, there is a holy relationship between being and feeling. When one opens the other, we perceive more deeply and understand more broadly. Just as thinking and feeling, together, can open the eyes of the deep, being and feeling, together, can unlock the heart to its heritage of compassion. You could say that being is a window into spirit, and that feeling is a window into our psychology. Yet while being will always open feeling, feeling can block being.

One way to understand our relationship to these things is to look at the sea. For each of us is like a great, untamed sea, obedient to deeper currents that are seldom visible. And just as the depth and surface of the sea are inseparable, so, too, are the spirit and psychology of each human being. Just as there is no way to discern where the deep stops and a wave begins, it is impossible to discern where the being of a person stops and where their feeling begins.

Empowering it all are the deep-sounding currents that cause us to rise and swell. We know these currents by many names: nature, life force, God, Tao, Atman, the breath of the Universe. Yet, for all of life's turmoil, that oceanic base of being remains unaffected by the storms that churn up the surface. It obeys a deeper order. This is another way to understand why meditation or stillness works, because it allows us to sink below the waves of our feelings into the clear depth of our being. Still, as spirits living in the world, we are always subject to both realms: the depth and the surface; our spirit and our psychology, our being and our feeling.

One of the daunting initiations into being is how we deal with pent-up feeling. Often, when bottled up, we live like a pressurized pipe. I know when I am hidden or closed, I so need to open up, to release that pressure, but I fear the bursting of all that unfelt being and feeling mounting within. This often keeps me from the very thing that will heal me. Even taking that initial risk, some of us are traumatized by this powerful release, and so we fear being and feeling, forever associating it with this terrible bursting from within. Ironically, though, like a pipe that has been opened, the heart will calm to a trickle and find its natural flow, if allowed to stay open. But this, you say, defeats the purpose of a pipe. True, a pipe is made to force water to flow in a certain direction, to force it to move from here to there. But for a person, there is a great cost for such forcing. So, here, the exquisite risk is to give up all forced direction and to allow our hearts, once opened, to find their natural flow.

This can be as difficult as it is necessary. Recently, a friend overheard two coal miners resting at the end of a long day. The older one broke the silence by saying, "You know, the most exciting thing for me is when we're working on a tunnel from both ends and we finally break through." The younger jumped in, "Yeah, it's that light coming through." "Yeah," the older one echoed, "it's mighty satisfying."

Often, the work of being and feeling is like the work of tunneling. It takes a great, sustained effort and faith that we will eventually break through to where others are tunneling. And it's all for that exciting, satisfying moment when nothing remains in the way, that moment when light comes through. This is an apt description for the journey from alienation to love. It gives a clear picture of how personal transformation can lead us, unknowingly, to others.

So I'd like to touch on some of the ways that feeling can block being, and speak to some of what we need to tunnel through—in ourselves and between each other. At least these are the places I've had to dig.

The first has to do with a confusion about our makeup as human beings. When I first tripped fully into the depth of being, I was intoxicated with the precious possibility of everything being so near and vital that I couldn't see and feel and experience enough. While the impulse for this was an innocent wonder, it was a quiet arrogance that worked its way with me.

I suffered what I call *experience greed*: the assumption that we can do it all. This points to the paradox of living as a human being: The being is infinite, but the human is finite. The nature of life is endless, but the life we live has limits. I struggled with this for a long time. I wanted so badly to experience and understand *everything!* But giving over to this growing, inner appetite, I had trouble experiencing and understanding *anything!* I constantly felt like I was missing something. And so I was seldom able to be where I was. Only when forced to accept that I couldn't experience everything, only when collapsing before the moment, did the moment offer everything.

But there was a deeper assumption here that was misleading me. It was the seductive sense that life is divided into moments that are special and ordinary. And somehow, if I was to grow, I had to sort the special from the ordinary and then pursue it. In this, I was truly misguided. For life is not a vertical climb through some specially marked path that will take us to some secret garden. It is, more beautifully, horizontal. Like a stone rippling in a lake, the heart of our being dropped softly into any moment will ripple us into the mystery of everything.

Once I finally grasped this, I realized what now seems obvious: that life is always *here*, and *here* is always beneath *there*. This became clear to me while on vacation one summer. I remember sitting for a long time on the edge of a lake, watching the far shore. I could see early light flood the water in the distance and this somehow made the other side seem exotic. Every morning, I'd sit on my small edge of lake and watch the other side, imagining that a certain mystery awaited me there. With each day its call grew larger. Finally, on the seventh day, I had to go there. Up earlier than usual, I rowed across the lake, beached my small boat, and sat in the exact spot I had been watching.

As I looked about, the aura of otherness I had seen from my daily perch was gone. I was somewhat undone, for though this far shore was beautiful and peaceful, the wet clump of earth I ran my hand through was the same as where I'd begun.

I started to laugh at myself. For looking back at where I'd been sitting every day, I saw early light flood the water in the distance, and now where I'd been seemed exotic. Now a certain mystery called me back to where I'd been.

So often we imagine that *there* is more full of gold than *here*. It is the same with love and dreams and the work of our lives. We see the light everywhere but where we are, and chase after what we think we lack, only to find, humbly, it was with us all along.

It is a challenging practice, but by accepting our limitations, we are forced to find life where we are. And in the mysterious space that opens before us, we begin to sense the specialness already in everything from the broken ladder to the bud of a rose three days from breaking ground. In actuality, each moment is pregnant with the fundamental truth that life is not calling from the corner of our eye, but is everywhere at once, waiting for us to enter. All that being said, to openly engage the life of our being and feeling is an active physic that returns us to that place inside that doesn't change.

After decades of struggling with being and feeling, the great poet Stanley Kunitz puts it this way, in his poem "The Layers":

> I have walked through many lives,
> some of them my own,
> and I am not who I was,
> though some principle of being
> abides, from which I struggle
> not to stray.

It is that abiding sense of being that helped me stay alive. When I stopped running from death and stopped chasing life, that abiding sense showed up like the strong friend that it is. And the days since have been vivid. For I have held the dying, have felt their life surge one last time like a surf, have held those not even a day old, have seen their eyes flicker out of focus at the coolness of this thing called air, and I have been the dying, held until I came back.

I have been crushed to center and left for invisible, and played like a sweet thing with broken strings, and in the hush after truth is shared, in the wake of all explanation and excuse, in the aftermath of illusions snapped like sticks, nothing matters now but the instant where all I am mounts like a wave for you. Nothing but the instant my hand parts the air between us. I tell you I have come so close to death that I forgot my name and now all names seem useless.

So nothing matters but emptying, until the softness we call spirit bubbles through the tongue and words fail in utter adoration. Nothing now but this need to be . . . naked in the midst of what we feel.

# GOING BEYOND

*O you need to say yes a lot!*

—Naomi Shihab Nye

I have an old friend who is slowly losing her hearing. At first I would notice her straining to pick up pieces of conversation. Like most of us, she was accustomed to a lifetime of language, so much so that there was this urgency in her face each time she felt that something meaningful had dropped like a stone into the canyon of her unwanted silence. I felt for her and it stirred my own fears of being her someday.

But something quietly amazing happened along the way. As she accepted her loss of hearing, as she lived into it more and more, I began to notice that she was more relaxed in group settings. She didn't strain anymore. I wondered if she had found a good hearing aid or if she just gave up on conversation. When I asked her about all this, it turned out it was neither.

We were walking in early spring and she explained, "It was horrible at first. You're right. I felt so left out. I've always been such a good listener, and now it's beyond how much I try or care. The essence sometimes slips right through into a silence I can't make sense of."

"But something's changed, hasn't it? I mean, I can tell that you're more at peace with it all, for some reason."

She laughed. "You know me well. Yes, I've been forced to go beyond and listen below. One day I just got tired of straining so hard for all the words, and in my exhaustion, I settled on my sister's eyes as she was talking. It was then that I realized there are many things to listen to. When the words fell out of reach, I began to listen to eyes, to bodies, to gestures, to the face behind the face. I began to listen to the warmth coming from another." She closed her eyes and felt for my face and said, "I may no longer get what led you here, but I so receive the heart of it now."

She helped me understand that there are many languages that words only point to, many ways of knowing that the mind only traces. And all the languages together bring us to that vital place beyond knowledge, where the life of being and feeling lead.

Recently, another dear, old friend—a very articulate, experienced man who just turned ninety, a doctor turned painter—said to me, "I'm tired of words. It's all come down to the silence in between them . . . like light between objects . . . like the love between us." While all this could easily lead one to a contemplative vow of silence, I understand it more clearly as allowing our verbal and written language to recede a bit, so that all the other languages might come forward, so that together they all might bring us more fully into the embodiment of what life has to offer.

As well, a few years ago, I was blessed to be part of a Fellows Program at the Fetzer Institute. For three years, this program convened a group of twenty to thirty people from around the world. We met for several days three times a year. Interestingly, we were very good, early on, at invoking holy space through many different forms (meditation, yoga, dance, poetry, shamanic drumming, song, ritual). Each served as a threshold to a more honest speech between us. However, by the third year, quite unexpectedly, these other modes of being and expressing no longer *served* a deeper speech alone. Instead, each *became* a meaningful and beautiful speech unto itself, no longer serving the product of an articulated wisdom, but drawing us equally into the experience of a deeper truth.

I began to look into this. In doing so, I came across *The Secret Oral Teaching in Tibetan Buddhist Sects*. There, this interesting distinction is made:

> The most striking of the Tibetan Buddhist doctrines in the Secret Teachings concerns *the going beyond*. This doctrine is based on the concept of *Prajna Paramita*. The Tibetans have given the term *Prajna Paramita* a very different meaning from that attributed to it by Indian authors and their Western translators.
>
> According to the latter, *Prajna Paramita* means *excellent wisdom, the best, the highest wisdom*, whereas the Tibetans translate this concept as *going beyond wisdom*.

How we understand this makes a huge difference. For "excellent wisdom" implies a state of knowing that we aspire to fulfill or attain. This is more in keeping with a Greek sense of perfection. But a wisdom we are to *go beyond* implies that wisdom itself is a threshold that we are called to cross into a yet deeper experience of living. It implies that the deepest experience exists beyond the doorways that knowledge opens.

This changes everything. Consider the Buddhist virtues that Tibetans hold as sacred. In Western translation they are called *the excellent virtues*, aspects of living to aspire to. In the Tibetan translation, they are called *the virtues through which one must go*, beyond which one must live. Some of these virtues include kindness, patience, energy or effort, meditation or concentration of mind, and transcendent wisdom. For me, at least, these are much more compelling as learnings to journey through than as aspects of character I have to live up to.

This all confirms that our penchant for thinking and speaking in concepts and words is only one way into the depth-experience of life. And we don't have to go far to know this. For our suffering quickly breaks down what we think we know and have to say into a more authentic and humble taste of being and feeling. Still, what does this mean in a daily way? Well, since the word *educate* means "to draw out, to call forth what is already present," perhaps our journey through the days is one of self-education: of calling forth through experience that which is already present within us, until we find the world within us and ourselves in the world. And such a way demands that we listen to more than just what we think we have to say.

Perhaps this is how St. Francis could listen to birds, how Monet could listen to the light and the water converse over the stones at Etretat, and how Beethoven in his irrevocable silence could listen for the immense tide of what he later called the Ninth Symphony. But let's be clear. This is not a substitute for honest speech. This does not condone the codependency of a loved one who insists, "You should understand me and my needs without my having to say anything." No, this is more about seizing the best that words can offer and using that to go beyond. It is more about the clear and quiet field that waits on the other side of words: so powerful when it appears, that a shred of loose paper clinging to a building can have something important to say about the decisions that await, if we can listen in between our chatter and not pass it by.

Like my friend who is losing her hearing, I think I'm ready to receive the heart of it now. For whatever chance there is to go beyond our suffering, we each will need to say *yes* a lot. And if there is a chance to inhabit wonder, we each will need to listen to as many languages as we can. It's left me to meditate on light and waves and leaves and wind. It's made me ponder, If the sun thinks by radiating light, then is its language warmth? If the ocean thinks by undulating its mass of waves, then is its language wetness? If a tree thinks by converting light to sugar, then is its language the sprouting of leaves? And if the wind thinks by moving through everything unseen, then is its language how it bends us? It's made me realize that I am tired of only thinking like a man and pray for the courage to radiate, to undulate, to sprout, and to move through everything unseen.

So, all we've been exploring comes down to this. In the life of care, there is nothing to accomplish. Only endless things to care for. Nothing to be mastered. Only an effort to lean into everything that is alive. Nothing to regret in what has brought us this far. Only gratitude that, as human beings, our humanness is a constant cocoon that keeps shedding to reveal that small, luminous portion of Universal spirit which we are privileged to be guardians of in our brief time on earth. Beyond the virtues of knowledge, the gift of such care is that it opens the well of being that makes life bearable.

# ENTERING THE DAYS

*When I opened the eye*
*inside the eye*
*inside my mind*

*the day opened its fist*
*saying, it was you*
*who gave me hours*
*who made them fingers*
*who made them*
*close about you . . .*

## A SMALL FLAME

Nothing is solved on our journey, not in life or in a book. Rather, we are, through love and suffering, ushered into a wakeful living that clarifies and softens our experience into something irreducible and precious. I have said this many ways. But now, as we approach the end of our time together, it bears saying yet again. It all comes to putting down this book—or any book—and entering the day that is before you. Today. Here. Now. This is always an immediate call, both for me who writes this and for you who reads it.

I'm reminded of Thomas Kelly, a Quaker scholar, who in the 1930s spoke of a need to devote ourselves to a "continued renewed immediacy," rather than leaning on a memory of a recent divine

moment. This really challenged how I enter the days. For, frequently, I refer back to the last time my wife and I made sweet love,
or the last time I laughed with my oldest friend, or the last time the
moon parted the clouds to find my dark face. I certainly don't want
to lose these moments. But I hear what Kelly is pointing to. For
leaning on the past in order to *Be-Here-Now* reveals a lack of faith.
Such a stance assumes that the moment at hand will have nothing to
offer. So, rather than pushing off of the best of what's happened,
how can I dare to lean into the abundant moment *about* to happen?

How simple and profound. Yet why is this so difficult? Well, like
so many things that appear simple, there is a paradox at work.
During the years that Carl Jung was exploring the Unconscious,
before he knew it was the Unconscious, he had a dream in which
he was carrying a small flame, probably a candle, as he was walking into the wind. It felt imperative that he keep going, and yet he
had to cup his free hand to protect the small flame from going out.
At the same time, he had a sense of some dark figure following
him. This made him fearful and so he moved even faster into the
wind, which made the small flame flicker all the more.

He woke to realize that the small flame was the light of consciousness we each carry. It is the light of our soul, which we must
protect and keep alive as we move through our days. And the dark
figure darting behind him was his own shadow cast by the flicker
of his soul's small flame.

We each must experience and engage these profound dynamics
of living: We must protect and keep the small flame we carry from
being blown out, we must lean into the wind of our days, and we
must accept and not run from the shadow we cast for being
human. In some way, everything we've looked at speaks to these
holy charges of being alive.

The most important of these charges is, obviously, keeping the
small flame alive. For what good is it to move through the days if
the light of our soul is snuffed? Yet we have no choice but to move

into that wind of time and experience. The days like wind just keep coming. Slow enough, though, and the wind fuels the flame. Too fast and it goes out.

So running into the future can kill us. Likewise, if we don't accept our shadow as part of ourselves, we can run from our humanness in fear, like Jung in his dream. In this way, living in the past and denying our humanness can also snuff the flame. We are left, then, with the delicate task of keeping the small flame alive while entering the days, while washing the dishes and paying the bills. At the same time, we are challenged not to run from our own shadow as if it were some monster out to kill us.

In essence, attending that small flame is attending our most personal relationship with God. It enables everything else. In her novel *The Abyss*, Marguerite Yourcenar suggests that God *is* that small flame, and that part of the immense faith and majesty of creation is that God has made it so that *we*, small beings that we are, are entrusted with keeping *Him* from being snuffed:

> Possibly He is only a small flame in our hands, and we alone are the ones to feed and keep this flame alight . . .

This is a striking way of looking at things. But we don't have to debate the strength or fragility of God here. What's useful is this: Since God is in every small gesture and thing of this world, then with every small courage we mount to better live our lives, we keep God's flame alive. The Jungian analyst Donald Raiche speaks to this when he says:

> Depression is but one instance where we are called to shelter the living flame, [to keep it from being snuffed.] We also do it as parents renouncing the impulses to interfere in the lives of our children, as spouses declining opportunities to manipulate a partner, and as citizens participating in the community that con-

stitutes our civilization. [Indeed,] the guarding of the flame is a fitting metaphor for our conscious engagement in the process of individuation.

In honoring love and seeking truth, we are keepers of the flame. I often carry questions like small flames and find they are spoken to in the most unexpected places. Shortly after asking everyone about such a notion of God, I visited a dear friend in Washington, D.C., and asked her, too. She had never thought about it like this. But she recalled how one day, her eight-year-old came to her asking, "If God created all of us, who created God?" She took her daughter on her lap and stared off: "I don't really know, sweetheart." They sat there for a while, and then her little girl said with the clarity of innocence, "I think God created all of us with His hands so that we could then create His head and heart."

## WHY WE NEED EACH OTHER

In 1961, near the end of his miraculous life as a baseball legend and his miserable life as a human being, a depleted Ty Cobb confessed, "If I had the chance to live my life over, I'd do things a little different. . . . I'd have more friends."

I'm sure he never read this passage from Simone Weil:

> Nothing among human things
> has such power to keep our gaze
> fixed ever more intensely upon God
> than friendship.

The truth is that we all have a little Cobb and a little Weil in each of us, and it is very difficult to keep the small flame within alive all by ourselves. It is why we need each other. To understand this more fully, we return to Basho's student Kikakou, who in the 1600s in Japan wrote this haiku:

> A blind child
> guided by his mother,
> admires the cherry blossoms . . .

This very poignant moment opens a truth no one can escape. For we each take turns being the blind child, the guiding other, and the blossom, never really knowing which until we've learned what we are to learn. So often we search our days for the part we are to play. In what ways are we blind? In what ways are we the guide? In what ways are we the blossom itself? So, each day, upon opening the door and entering the world, we don't know what or who we will find and how they will help to complete us.

Along the way, we keep feeling for the one language we all share. It's interesting that, in the 1800s, a pidgin expression developed in the South Pacific—*wantok*. It was spoken by lonely sailors who, when docking in New Guinea, were hoping to meet someone who might speak their native tongue. They were desperate to speak directly with another, to need no intermediary, no translator. They wanted only a "one-talk."

Isn't this what we all want? Isn't this what we hope each day will bring? And isn't the *wantok* love? Frank Ostaseski, founder of the Zen Hospice Project in San Francisco, tells us that the most frequent question to rise from those who are dying is: Have I loved well? If nothing else, when you put down this book, carry this question: alone, in nature, when praying, when suffering.

I know, for me, it has taken half a century to cross some ocean in myself. And finally, what I feel is what I say and what I say is what I mean. What I mean is that others, so used to my gargantuan efforts to be good, don't understand my efforts to be real. They find me coming up short. But I'm simply burning old masks.

And the next step takes me—I don't know where—as it should be. I don't know: just that I love who I love. I listen with my heart. I struggle with the reflexes of my mind. And the pains of life are sharper now but disappear more clearly the way knives are swallowed by the sea. And the subtleties of being come on like waves that cleanse but which, when dry, cannot be seen.

So much like a gentle animal now, unsure what I was fighting for, except to breathe and sing, except to call out the human names of God that others have uttered when thoroughly stripped of their plans. So much like a love animal now until the end of any day's work is the soft moment when loving and being loved are the same. And all year round, the birds and trees instruct, make visible the wind, the way reaching without shame makes visible the love.

Even now, as I scratch these questions, Mira, our dog-child, now three, keeps nudging me to stop and be. And though we held her as a pup, she has a need to be held that comes from beyond us. Though I sat with her when she was the size of a loaf of bread, sat on the kitchen floor staring into each other's eyes, she has a need to stare that comes from a place beneath the awkwardness of humans. These days, she seems a furry, naked thing that never looks away.

Now I understand: God made the animals as raw, breathing elements, each closer in their way to one aspect of being. And that the friction of time on earth might have its chance to make us wise, God made the animals speechless. I keep remembering that Mira in Spanish means "to look." And lately, she licks us awake and stares deep into us, as if to say, *Get up. Don't look away. Admit you need to be held.*

So if you see me on the street, cupping something as I lean into the wind, don't be shy. Come over and help. For it's God I'm carrying, or at least that portion of God we call the soul. So come and help. And I will calm your fear of what's chasing you. And, perhaps, we can put whatever books we carry down, and open our small flames to the sun.

# WAITING FOR LIGHT

*I will lean and bow until*
*heaven is simply the appearance of light.*
*It will only come from holding things*
*that want to close open.*

We're getting close. Soon there will be nothing left to say. At least for now. So let's go deep, way deep, to the bottom of the Atlantic Ocean, where, thousands of feet below sea level, there are cracks in the crust of the earth's core. In this unbreakable darkness, the endless fire at the center of the earth seeps through these cracks, heating springs along the seafloor close to 750 degrees. Obviously, there is no light this far down.

Yet in 1985 marine biologists were surprised to find light-sensitive shrimp living near these springs. What could these tiny creatures possibly be sensing so far away from any source of light? With digital cameras, scientists photographed the seafloor springs, amazed to find "a dramatic, unequivocal glow."

This is yet more proof that everything is lighted from within. At center, we are all lighted, each of us carrying an unequivocal glow. And when feeling stranded on the bottom, completely in the dark, we can look to the center for some relief. For the powerful presence of life is seeping through our deepest cracks like a hidden sun.

Yes, even when we're stranded in the dark, this fire at the center—that quiet place beneath all names where we are joined to God—this fire is a deep and lasting friend. Estranged from this place, we suffer wounds that never stop. For without knowing who I am—that is, without finding the place where God and I join—I will become everyone I love. Without drinking from the quiet— that is, without listening for the place from which all living things speak—I will talk too much and wonder why I am not heard. Without seeking the self that lives beneath all names, all my attempts at kindness will fail, for everything I do will turn everyone in need into me. This being human is a series of blindnesses that come and go. But we can outlive our mistakes, for the mysterious fire at center is always near and greater than our need.

And like someone awakened to how they have hurt others through the years, like such a being who is now kinder and more giving, though those wounded along the way don't recognize this gentler person, we try harder and harder to live what is true until the truth wears us thin enough for light to come through. Like gravity, there seems to be some law of spiritual physics that works its magic over time. As Simone Weil says, "Even if our efforts of attention seem for years to be producing no result, one day a light that is in exact proportion to them will flood the soul."

In effect, we are cut and worn by experience and we polish what's left with the care and love of others until we are like stained glass—transparent patches of color waiting for light. Only if so worn and polished, so lived and practiced, do we illumine when light finds us, letting truth and spirit through. And though these enlightened moments are brief, they change everything.

In these moments, it is clear that the most underrated miracle of all is being human, and this journey to being transparent deeply affects how we relate to others. Consider what Osho says about being a master:

The Master is not a master over others, but a master of him or herself. And so welcomes others not because he or she wants to lead them, but because together, they create an energy field that supports each unique individual in finding his or her own light.

So there is something we can do while we wait. It involves *how* we receive what is light and what is dark, and helping each other prepare the skillful means for each. Earlier, we spoke of not-turning-one-thing-into-another as key to knowing things as they are. But, paradoxically, within that necessary and beautiful mind-set lies the best use of our will, which is the rightful turning of one thing into another.

There are two stories that are very helpful here. The one involves turning what is dark and toxic into water, and the other involves turning what is light and nourishing into food. In the science fiction classic *Dune*, by Frank Herbert, Jessica is the mother of a prophet foretold in the history of the people on this desert world. As a rite of validation that he is the prophet, she is required to drink a poison and retreat into a cave for three days. If she can survive, her son will be accepted as the legitimate seer to lead the people.

So Jessica retreats into the heart of the mountain, drinks the poison, and enters such a deep state of meditation that she is inside the very molecules of the Universe. There, inside the very elements that make up life, where things live beneath their names, she can see that what makes this liquid that she drank a poison is that its elements are connected in a particular way. She concentrates her entire being to where the poison is pooling within her body, and with all her energy of heart and mind, she nudges one element so that the particles of the poison are connected differently. Once in different relationship, the elements no longer form a poison. Once doing this, she relinquishes her will as the poison turns to water and she returns to a more normal state of meditation. And then she wakes.

This moment is a compelling metaphor for the transformative moment in our daily lives. It reveals a telling way that we might participate in turning what is poisonous in our lives into something more simple and ordinary. Now, try as I will, I can't change the molecules in the things before me. But I can enter the storm of conflict that surrounds me—in myself, in my relationships, in the culture that exists where I live—I can enter its very living structure until I can see which out-of-balance element is making the situation poisonous. And then I can nudge it, can guide it until it is in different relationship to the elements around it. I can, through my full and conscious being, render it harmless. I can do so in myself, in my past, in the poison of my wounds, in the wounds of my society. It may not always work. It may not always be possible. But if we can lean in and look this closely at fear, distrust, envy, and self-centeredness, we might be able to find the one particular eating us up inside that makes these conditions toxic.

It took years for me to realize that to run from something toxic and dark, especially within, only enlarges it. Rather, we need to lean into it, to enter what we fear is poisonous till we can see what it is made of. Often, this deep and honest seeing is enough to shift its elements. And chances are that once its elements are in different relationship, it will no longer be poisonous.

While this helps us break down what is destructive, it doesn't show us how to incorporate what is healing and abundant. This leads us to the second story, which is the way of photosynthesis: how plants turn light into sugar. We are all taught the mechanics of this in school. But the miracle of it is that plants are the only creatures that can turn light into food. Open this in your mind till you can see the pure fact of it. It is the aspiration of every contemplative practice on earth, the hope of every attempt to love: to live off the presence of life that surrounds us. Every painful form of loneliness and lack of worth comes from the soul being cut off from everything life-giving, as if some clear wall is sealing us from being touched. Often, in this state, we run desperately from misadventure to misadventure, all in an urgent attempt not to go completely numb. All the while, the smallest fern, unable to go anywhere, simply opens itself and lives off the day. It does this by receiving light through its leaves and mixing it with water drawn from its roots, turning the presence of that light into sugar which keeps the plant alive. For us, this means continually trying to receive the mysterious presence of life into our heart, where it can turn into a precious form of sugar that can keep us alive and sweeten our blood.

I don't know how these two miracles work, and though I struggle myself to access them, the image of them helps me work toward what is possible. Together, they form a crucial practice for the rightful use of our will: the turning of what is poisonous into something simple to drink, and the turning of what is abundant and mysterious into food. And who knows. Perhaps in forty or fifty generations, we, like Jessica, will be able to enter the heart of the mountain and from way deep inside turn the poison into water. Perhaps in time, such skillful means will be taught as part of a spiritual literacy we've yet to understand. It might be the medicine of the future.

As it is, we, like every generation before us, are blessed from time to time to glimpse the mystery. It comes through in spite of our constant misperceptions. Rob Lehman puts it this way: "The great blind spot in human history is that we so often see life as separate and alien when it is truly being woven together in love. It is the occasional glimpse of this weaving that the Christian calls *Christ Consciousness,* and the Buddhist, *Enlightenment.*"

If we live long enough, these glimpses have their way with us. It is a humble goal of spiritual practice to be worn through enough, so that, as Huston Smith puts it, "these flashes of illumination gradually become the abiding light." In this, each of us is a flower tucked into itself and covered thinly in order to grow. But once we've grown, the light over time burns a hole in our covering here and another hole there, until after enough burnings, the covering falls away, and we blossom. I imagine the journey to enlightenment has a similar feel. Once worn through, by love or suffering, the soft task might be simply to blossom and wear light.

I have been burned open many times and, in truth, it's been hard sometimes to know which burnings have been providential and which just sheer suffering. But lately there is more space around my words and I suspect what is true waits between my utterance and its echo. If you look here, the way you might follow a thread of sun through a break in the undergrowth, I think you will understand. Like Lazarus, I am calm only because I've already died and this life after life is so ordinary it is raw. Touch me when I am fully here and we just might ignite into a faceless joy.

# THE GIFT AND
# THE SADDLE

*You didn't come into this house so I might tear off
a piece of your life. Perhaps when you leave
you'll take something of mine: chestnuts, roses or
a surety of root[s . . . ]*

—PABLO NERUDA

One of my favorite images comes from Basho. In 1689 he is walking around the Island of Japan and doesn't know the way. He asks a farmer, who says, "It's easier if you just take my horse. He knows the way. When you get to the next town, just let him go and he'll come home." So Basho is led by this majestic creature and, once at the next town, he ties a gift to the empty saddle and sends the horse home. That image of the riderless horse with a gift tied to its empty saddle touches me. Perhaps because I've been lost so many times over the years. Perhaps because I've been quietly saved by the kindness of strangers. Perhaps because some of my most satisfying moments as a human being have risen from the anonymous giving that we are sometimes called to offer. Perhaps because being a spirit in the world is so much like following a riderless horse that we lose and share and return to each other.

I do know that the more centered I become, the more I realize that I am not the center, and that love is not arrived at but lived.

And so I believe that birth is not a gate left open behind us, but an ongoing awakening—in which the sincere and honest moment is a temple with no doors.

We have time for one more story, which comes from the vast mythology of Gabriel Garcia Marquez. It goes like this. Somewhere, in a time like our own, a father is pensively trying to solve the world's problems when his little boy comes in and says, "Father, I want to help." The weary man appreciates the gesture but only feels the child's presence as a hindrance. But the boy persists. So the father takes a map of the world and rips it into little pieces, gives them to the boy, and says, "I know you like puzzles. You can help by piecing the world back together." The boy protests, "But Father, I don't even know what the world looks like!" His father laughs, "Nonetheless, this is how you can help," and he sends him off, expecting that this will occupy his son for days.

And so the pensive man returns to his weary reflections. Two days later, his son comes bounding in, shouting, "Father! Father! I've put the world back together!" And sure enough, all the torn pieces are taped into a beautiful whole. His father is stunned. "But how did you do this?"

The boy is eager to show him and turns the map of the world over, saying, "On the back was a picture of a person, Father. I put the person back together and then turned it over and the world was back together!"

This simple story carries the profound wisdom that when we put ourselves back together, we put the world back together. That each of our unfathomable journeys is a torn piece in the living puzzle that is the world. That each time we take the exquisite risk toward being whole, toward living in the open, toward recognizing and affirming that we are, at heart, each other, we put the world back together. The truth is that each of our struggles matters, and we need each other to turn the story of our lives over to see how they so beautifully go together. Isn't all our work about the picture of the person and the picture of the world and how the thousand torn pieces wait to be joined?

You see, this is how wisdoms make love and give birth to truths that can help. I have carried Basho's story for years, and now that I've heard about the boy and the map of the world, I understand that each time we tie a gift to the saddle, we put one piece of our selves and the world back together.

I have to say, I find it hard to end this book, because the river it rides never ends. My heart is full of voices and their song is nearing the edge of silence. It is not that the song ends, but more, our ability to praise it into being gets exhausted and the song sails on—waiting for the next circus of yearning spirits to bring it back to life. For now, accept this book of praise as my gift tied to the saddle. And when it's your turn, tie something dear to the empty saddle and send the horse on its way.

# NOTES

MOVEMENT 1. THERE ARE TEACHERS EVERYWHERE

## Listening to the Voice Inside

3 *If I dare to hear you* Unless otherwise noted, the epigraphs throughout are written by the author.

## The Exquisite Risk

A draft version of this section was first published in *Sufi: A Journal of Sufism*. London: Khaniqahi Nimatullahi Publications, Issue 57, Spring 2003.

14 *The exquisite risk to still our own house* This quote is from *Dark Night of the Soul: St. John of the Cross*, translated by Mirabai Starr. New York: Riverhead Books, 2002, p. 33. It is a paraphrase of the lines:

> O exquisite risk!—
> Undetected I slipped away.
> My house, at last, grown still.

## The Strange Storyteller

17 *Say it. Say it. The Universe is made of stories, not atoms* From Muriel Rukeyser's poem "The Speed of Darkness," in *The Longman Anthology of Contemporary American Poetry*, edited by Stuart Friebert and David Young. New York: Longman, 1989, 2d ed., p. 122.

## You Must Reverse the Haiku

21 *We shouldn't abuse God's creatures* From *George Seferis: A Poet's Journal, 1945–1951*, translated by Athan Anagnostopoulos. Cambridge, Mass.: Harvard University Press, 1974, p. 59.

23 *If you are kind, people* From *Anyway: The Paradoxical Commandments, Finding Personal Meaning in a Crazy World*, Kent Keith. New York: G. P. Putnam's Sons, 2002.

24 *If you don't know the kind of person I am* From the poem "A Ritual to Read to Each

Other," in *The Way It Is: New & Selected Poems*, William Stafford. St. Paul, Minn.: Graywolf Press, 1998, p. 75.

24 *So, drawn on by my destiny* From "The Poet's Obligation," in *The Selected Poems*, *Pablo Neruda*, edited by Nathaniel Tarn. New York: Dell Publishing, 1972, p. 428.

## Fame and Peace

30 *I want to be famous in the way a pulley is famous* From "Famous," in *Words Under the Words: Selected Poems*, Naomi Shihab Nye. Portland, Ore.: Eighth Mountain Press, 1995, p. 80.

## The Struggle to Be Real

A draft version of this section was first published in *Sufi: A Journal of Sufism*. London: Khaniqahi Nimatullahi Publications, Issue 58, Summer 2003.

## A Sincere Life

A draft version of this section was first published in *Sufi: A Journal of Sufism*. London: Khaniqahi Nimatullahi Publications, Issue 56, Winter 2003.

51 *If you ask people in India why* From a sermon on Gandhi delivered in Montgomery, Alabama, on March 22, 1959. In *The Autobiography of Martin Luther King, Jr.*, edited by Clayborne Carson. New York: Warner Books, 1998, p.128.

## There Are Teachers Everywhere

A draft version of this section was first published in *Sufi, A Journal of Sufism*. London: Khaniqahi Nimatullahi Publications, Issue 60, Winter 2004.

## MOVEMENT 2. STEERING OUR WAY TO CENTER

### Steering Our Way to Center

70 *A fish cannot drown in water* From *The Enlightened Heart*, edited by Stephen Mitchell. New York: Harper & Row, 1989.

73 *As rivers flowing into the ocean* From *The Upanishads*, translated by Juan Mascaro. London: Penguin, 1965.

### Giving and Getting Attention

90 *I should be content* From *News of the Universe: Poems of Twofold Consciousness*, edited by Robert Bly. San Francisco, Calif.: Sierra Club Books, 1980, p. 123.

91 *Like a human microscope* It is interesting that while Monet and Van Gogh were looking so deeply into nature, the microscope itself was being developed elsewhere in Europe.

NOTES

281

92 *All of us, whether we are blind or not* From *And There Was Light*, Jacques Lusseyran. New York: Parabola Books, 1987, pp. 27–28.

## The Gift of Surprise

117 *Not I, but the wind that blows through me* From *The Selected Poems of D. H. Lawrence*. New York: Viking Press, 1959, p. 74.

## The Life of Expression

122 *It is not by accident that Native American medicine men put these questions to the sick* These insights are preserved by the cultural anthropologist Angeles Arrien, whose landmark book, *The Four-Fold Way*, synthesizes indigenous wisdom from around the world.

124 *I come to you from a land where elders . . . will outlast brutality* This passage is part of a larger journal of my time in South Africa called "Where the HeartBeast Sings," which was first published in *Sufi: A Journal of Sufism*. London: Khaniqahi Nimatullahi Publications, Issue 38, Spring 1998, pp. 22–33.

### MOVEMENT 3. HOW CAN WE GO THERE TOGETHER?

#### How Can We Go There Together?

140 *René Lenoir tells us* From *Les Exclus*, René Lenoir. Paris: Editions du Seuil, 1974. In *Community and Growth*, Jean Vanier, pp. 15–16.

141 *The mythic Chien of China* From *Mathews' Chinese-English Dictionary*. Cambridge, Mass.: Harvard University Press, 1960, p. 114.

#### The Spoked Wheel

145 *We join spokes together in a wheel* This version of Chapter 11 in The Tao is a hybrid of two translations: *Tao Te Ching*, translated by Stephen Mitchell (New York: Harper & Row, 1988, p. 11), and *Tao Teh Ching*, translated by John C. Wu (Boston: Shambhala Press, 1989, p. 23).

#### The Song of Relationship

150 *The ancient Egyptians regarded relationship as an art* Again, I am indebted to Angeles Arrien for her deep knowledge of the peoples of the world.

#### The Loss of One Brick

154 *We must love one another or die* From "Septemb̶ ̶ ̶ ̶ ̶ ̶ Poems, W. H. Auden, edited by Edward Mendel̶ ̶

## The Feather of Truth

161 *The "Trial of Heart" ceremony that Egyptians believed every person faced at the end of their life* From *Heart,* Gail Godwin. New York: William Morrow, 2001, pp. 27–30.

## The Rhythm of Kindness

166 *As Mencius says* Mencius was the grandson of Confucius, a respected philosopher in his own right.

167 *The* Kindertransport *Into the Arms of Strangers* is an inspiring documentary (2001) that chronicles the stories of the children brought to England out of Germany during 1938 and 1939.

169 *Go to the pine if you want to learn* From *George Seferis: A Poet's Journal, 1945–1951,* translated by Athan Anagnostopoulos. Cambridge, Mass.: Harvard University Press, 1974, p. 106.

## The Eyes of the Deep

A draft version of this section was first published in *Sufi: A Journal of Sufism.* London: Khaniqahi Nimatullahi Publications, Issue 59, Fall 2003.

173 *The fishermen of Colombia created the word* sentipensante From *The Book of Embraces,* Eduardo Galeano. New York: W. W. Norton & Co., 1989. Laura Rendon, at California State University–Long Beach, has developed a wonderful curriculum for educators based on *sentipensante.*

174 *[It is] an attitude of life* From *Dark Wood to White Rose: The Journey of Transformation in Dante's Divine Comedy,* Helen M. Luke. New York: Parabola Books, 1989, p. 77.

176 *So, through me, freedom and the sea* From "The Poet's Obligation," in *The Selected Poems of Pablo Neruda,* translated by Alastair Reid. New York: Delta Books, 1972, p. 428.

## The Stripping of Our Will

191 *I live my life in growing orbits* This version is a hybrid of two translations: *Selected Poems of Rainer Maria Rilke,* translated by Robert Bly (New York: Harper & Row, 1981), p. 13, and *Ahead of All Parting: The Selected Poetry and Prose of Rainer Maria Rilke,* translated by Stephen Mitchell (New York: The Modern Library, 1995), p. 5.

## MOVEMENT 4. HONORING THE MYSTERY

### Honoring the Mystery

208 *The purpose of affirmation* From *Dynamics of Living,* Charles Fillmore. Unity Village, Mo.: Unity Books, 1967, p. 66.

## Things As They Are

215 *There's a thread you follow* From *The Way It Is: New & Selected Poems*, William Stafford. St. Paul, Minn.: Graywolf Press, 1998, p. 42.

221 *Hoping for beauty* From "A Farewell Gift to Sora," in *Basho's Narrow Road*, translated by Hiroaki Sato. Berkeley, Calif.: Stone Bridge Press, 1996, p. 163.

222 *Is-ness is God* From *Start Where You Are*, Pema Chodron. Boston: Shambhala Press, 1994, p. 89.

## Heaven on Earth

225 *For the raindrop, joy is entering the lake* From *Nine Gates: Entering the Mind of Poetry*, Jane Hirshfield. New York: HarperCollins Publishers, 1997, p. 5.

225 *For those who have found the still point of eternity* From *Oriental Mythology*, Joseph Campbell. New York: Penguin, 1976, p. 3.

229 *One thing is made up of all other things* From *Going Home: Jesus and Buddha as Brothers*, Thich Nhat Hanh. New York: Riverhead Books, 1999, p. 5.

## At the Pace of What Is Real

233 *The Jungian analyst Helen Luke* Helen's work is a remarkable map to the inner geography we all face. She speaks to Ulysses and the oar in her book *Old Age: Journey into Simplicity* (New York: Parabola Books, 1987). Another invaluable book of hers is *Dark Wood to White Rose: The Journey of Transformation in Dante's Divine Comedy* (New York: Parabola Books, 1989), which is as far from literary criticism as you can get. These books changed my life.

## In Flawed Abundance

237 *The abundance of life is always present* From *Dynamics of Living*, Charles Fillmore. Unity Village, Mo.: Unity Books, 1967, p. 254.

238 *"Be you perfect" really means "be you all-embracing"* This is from an amazing book, *Prayers of the Cosmos: Meditations on the Aramaic Words of Jesus*, translated by Neil Douglas-Klotz. Calif.: HarperSanFrancisco. 1990.

239 *It is through self-knowledge* From "Preface," by Aldous Huxley in *The First and Last Freedom*, Krishnamurti. Calif.: HarperSanFrancisco, 1954, p. 12.

240 *The major failures of our time* From *A Hidden Wholeness: The Journey Toward an Undivided Life*, Parker J. Palmer. San Francisco, Calif.: Jossey-Bass, 2004.

## Chores

An earlier version of this section was first published in *Pilgrimage: Reflections on the Human Journey*, vol. 20, no. 1, Jan./Feb. 1994, pp. 25–28.

### Being and Feeling

257 *I have walked through many lives* From *The Poems of Stanley Kunitz, 1928–1978*. Boston, Mass.: Little, Brown & Co., 1979, p. 35.

### Going Beyond

261 *The most striking of the Tibetan Buddhist doctrines* From *The Secret Oral Teaching in Tibetan Buddhist Sects*, Alexandra David-Neel and Lama Yongden. San Francisco, Calif.: City Lights Books, 1967, pp. 74–76.

### Entering the Days

266 *Possibly He is only a small flame in our hands* From *The Abyss*, Marguerite Yourcenar. pp. 220–222.

266 *Depression is but one instance* From "A Small Flame in Our Hands," Donald Raiche, in *Sufi: A Journal of Sufism*. London: Khaniqahi Nimatullahi Publications, Issue 60, Winter 2004.

### Waiting for Light

270 *A dramatic, unequivocal glow* From National Undersea Research Program, in *Awake!*, November 22, 2000.

### The Gift and the Saddle

276 *You didn't come into this house* From "Wine," in *Selected Poems, Pablo Neruda*, edited by Nathaniel Tarn. New York: Dell Publishing, 1972, p. 275.

# GRATITUDES

There are many to thank. Some I know and some I don't. But all have graced me with the inspiration of their humanity, with the courage of their own exquisite risks to be here, to stay here, to help others along the way. To the Fetzer Institute, which continues to be such a deep home for me. And to my colleagues for encouraging me to be who I am by sharing who they are, and to my friends for always leading me to the holy well that waits between us when we dare to love. To Wayne Muller, whose kindness and friendship is a continual oasis. To Parker Palmer, who encouraged me to build a house of vision that anyone could enter. To Loretta Barrett, my agent, whose heart is as wide as her eye is keen—what a gardener you are, your belief watered and pruned this book to grow. To Teryn Johnson, who first welcomed this book with such good will. To Julia Pastore, my editor, for keeping the well-being of the book at the center of our conversations. To my spirit-brother, Robert, we have tumbled so far that it feels like we're flying. And to my wife, Susan, your deep risk to love heals. And to our dog-child, Mira, whose entire being is one huge gratitude licking and sniffing in every direction. And to Grandma, who came to this country that I should find the country within. All I seem to do now is enter the days, looking for love, in order to ask the simplest of questions. It is a good life, and I feel deep gratitude for the wisdom of so many people who, quietly and unexpectedly, have shared their stories and their truth. We are more together than alone.

# PERMISSIONS

Thanks for permission to excerpt from the following previously published works:

# ABOUT THE AUTHOR

Mark Nepo is a poet and philosopher who has taught in the fields of poetry and spirituality for thirty years. Nominated for the Lenore Marshall Poetry Prize, he has written several books, including *The Book of Awakening*, *Acre of Light* (also available as an audiotape from Parabola under the title *Inside the Miracle*), *Fire Without Witness*, and *God, the Maker of the Bed, and the Painter*. He has also contributed to numerous anthologies. *The Book of Awakening* was a finalist for the 2000 Books for a Better Life Award and was cited by *Spirituality and Health Magazine* as one of the Best Spiritual Books of 2000. Mark is also the editor of *Deepening the American Dream: Reflections on the Inner Life and Spirit of Democracy*, a collection of essays. His most recent books of poetry are *Suite for the Living* and *Inhabiting Wonder*. These poetry books and a CD of Mark's poetry, *Finding Our Way in the World*, are available from Bread for the Journey (www.breadforthejourney.org). As well, *Unlearning Back to God*, a collection of Mark's published essays from 1985 to 2005, has been recently published by Khaniqahi Nimatullahi Publications. A new book of poetry and prose, *Surviving Has Made Me Crazy*, is due out from CavanKerry Press (www.CavanKerryPress.org) in February 2007. His work has been translated into French, Portuguese, Japanese, and Danish.

As a cancer survivor, Mark remains committed to the usefulness of daily inner life. Through both his writing and his teaching, he devotes himself to the life of inner transformation and relationship, exploring the expressive journey of healing where the paths of art and spirit meet. For eighteen years, Mark taught at the State University of New York at Albany. He now serves as a Program Officer for the Fetzer Institute in Kalamazoo, Michigan, a non-profit foundation devoted to fostering awareness of the power of love and forgiveness in the emerging global community. He continues to give readings, lectures, and retreats.